WHAT PEOPLE ARE SAYING...

One of the top 2 books K-von has ever written!

~*Amazon*

After reading this, I no longer feel the need to travel.

~*Recluse*

Can't afford to take my girl on vacation, so bought her this book instead. Same thing!

~*Frat Guy*

I now live by the motto: "Beware of Bangkok."

~*Businessman*

It's hard to believe one comedian has travelled this much and I've never heard of him.

~*New Fan*

This is sure to become a best-seller on a lesser known list.

~*NY Times*

Written during Covid-19 Pandemic, but carefully disinfected.

~*Leading Epidemiologist*

Finally, a book free of politics that somehow offends both the 'left' & 'right' equally.

~*RNC & DNC Joint Press Statement*

ONCE YOU GO EVERYWHERE

TRAVEL THE WORLD WITH THE
MOST FAMOUS 1/2 PERSIAN COMEDIAN

K-VON MOEZZI

First Printing, 2024

ISBN 979-8-35090-306-5
eBook ISBN 979-8-35090-307-2

Cover photos by Leavitt Wells | @leaveittoleavitt

TANX GOD! PRODUCTIONS
WWW.K-VONCOMEDY.COM

CONTENTS

THE TRAVEL PARADOX

You have TIME to travel, but no MONEY.
You start making MONEY, and no longer have the TIME.
You finally have the TIME & MONEY, but no longer have
the ENERGY.

It's been my lifelong goal to beat this conundrum and I encourage you to do the same. Don't put off a well-deserved trip. Find a way to make it happen. For instance, I've been to Europe five times:

> **Low Budget:** *as a poor college kid*
>
> **Middle Class:** *on an all-expense-paid company trip*
>
> **Taken:** *as a "plus-one" for a wedding*
>
> **Single:** *by myself for a quick getaway*
>
> **Comedian:** *on a fun tour*

Visiting the exact same cities at different periods in life provided wildly different experiences. Turns out my budget had very little to do with the amount of fun I had, or the memories made. (In fact, sparser circumstances often led to better stories.)

Be sure to check dream destinations off your list no matter where you are in life. Don't wait for the *perfect* time to explore the world, because it may never come.

INTRODUCTION

People often joke, "My life is sooo crazy, I should totally write a book about it!" But high-performance individuals don't just say stupid things, we follow through with them – so here it is. In my previous book, *Once You Go Persian,* we discussed my upbringing, made fun of my family, and detailed how one becomes a standup comedian.

This picks up right where that one left off, discussing even more of my upbringing and making even more fun of my family. You may not know it, but I was once on a standard path to great success. I graduated at the top of my class, became a thriving sales rep, even accepted into law school – then threw it all away to become a comedian... *Who does that?!*

The question I get most, "What made you decide to get into comedy?" In reality, I wanted to be in a boy band but didn't have three other cute friends. I also couldn't sing that well, dancing was a struggle, and my frosted tips never came out quite right. This left me with no other choice but to pursue something solo. Another question, "Was everyone always telling you how funny you were?" Quite the opposite – anyone who truly loved me tried to persuade me out of comedy. (To this day, I'm still suspicious of those who supported the idea back then.) To the best of anyone's memory I'd never been funny. An opinion thousands of online commenters along with my mother still hold to this day. (It just occurred to me, she may be the one who keeps writing, "Dis dude is wack!" under all those various screen names.)

The past 15 years, I've toured the world non-stop in an attempt to prove them all wrong.

The verdict is still out, but one thing is undeniable: I've picked up a lot of valuable skills and enjoyed some wild adventures along the way. Traveling at this capacity is an art, and I didn't realize how good at it I'd become until recently bringing a rookie along for the ride.

A buddy of mine joined me on a trip and looked like a bumbling fool at every turn. We arrived at the airport and he had no idea what to do or where to go. Instead of a rolling suitcase, he carried his clothes along with his lunch in a repurposed plastic shopping bag. Check-in was a hassle and by the time he got to the other side of the security checkpoint, we'd almost missed our flight. He had his pants around his ankles, one arm out of his jacket, had lost his phone, and discovered there was now a hole in his bag. He was receiving an additional pat-down by the TSA while spilling his personal belongings on the floor. What took him hours, I was doing in seconds. Simple things like:

- walking *beep-less* through the airport metal detector
- lifting the arm on the plane's aisle seat for ease of exit (*yes, most have a button for that*)
- sneaking a bottle of water past security
- and many more...

It occurred to me he likely wasn't alone. By sharing a lot of this information, I could make you into an expert road warrior as well. Novice travelers pay overpriced parking fees at hotels, never get their own row on airplanes, they *buy* breakfast instead of finding a hotel that offers it for free... the list goes on. There was a movie with George Clooney called *Up in The Air*. I watched in disbelief. They'd basically made a documentary about my life without permission. I had no idea this was enough fodder for a major Hollywood film and now had no royalties to show for it! Since they left out all the really good parts, I decided to add them back in right here. In the following pages, I'll provide travel hacks, tips, tricks, and stories from an international funny man. I don't recommend you try them all, as many are morally questionable (and some downright illegal). I'm out here taking big risks, so you don't have to. Imagine James Bond. Now replace his fancy wardrobe with H&M, replace his handgun with a microphone, and replace his bank account with coupons – and you've got "von... K-von".

For the first time I'll share personal stories, dating tales, dangerous liaisons, brushes with the law, major regrets, and two near death experiences from my whirlwind travels. It's all here in a collection of snippets that will leave you shaken, not stirred.

*Now please put your tray tables up, sit back, relax, and get ready... we're about to take off.

CHAPTER 1: BEDTIME

I'm typing this while lying on a plush bed in a luxurious hotel overlooking Manhattan – my current "office" for the week. One of the perks of being a comedian. I'm not bragging. Last week it was a run-down motel in Montana. I can appreciate both.

It's uncomfortable for me to sit for long periods of time at my desk because, well– *I'M OLD*. I may look like the "½ Persian Justin Bieber of Comedy" but I have the "Morgan Freeman of back pain".

My previous job, medical device sales, provided a company car with unlimited miles and a gas card. That was a great benefit, and for a guy on a budget it meant every vacation was going to be "driving distance". For years, I'd cut out of work early on Friday, hop in that Chrysler 300, and cruise as far as possible to check out a new destination.

As long as I was back by Monday-ish, nobody at the office seemed to care. I logged approximately 50,000 miles a year, driving wherever those four little tires would take me.

There I was, 26 years old with a surging pain going down my right leg. "I'm too young for this!" I would scream. My sciatic nerve disagreed. During that time, I bought every ice pack, back pillow, cream, and do-it-yourself-acupressure-ball I could find. I changed my chair, my mattress, my vehicle... even my girlfriend – nothing seemed to work. Doctors recommended I stop driving so often but that interfered with my strategy. This was my vacation-mobile and there was still so much to see. Work was getting in the way of my adventures, and that pain was one of the reasons I left the corporate world for good. I needed a job less intense that maximized travel. Comedy was the answer, and nothing is more laid-back than *Standup Comedian*. I mean, at this point I've switched positions and am now typing this while literally *LAYING-BACK!*

A little side-story: at my sales job they'd have us come to corporate headquarters for training. I'm a runner so I'd wake up at 5am and hit the pavement for up to 10 miles before work. One morning they dimmed the lights to play a video, so I very discreetly slid my leather shoes off under the table (after all, my feet were BURNING from the jog). Once the video ended, my leather loafers were back on before the lights were. Later that day I was called into the office, "Did you take your shoes off this morning during the training video?"

"Umm, well, yea for a moment, but it was dark in there. Who-"

"Listen, you're already the youngest guy in this company. People are looking for you to screw up, and you just did. Make sure it never happens again."

Who was so focused on *my feet* to even notice? We should write THAT GUY up since he obviously wasn't paying attention to the video! Out of twenty sales reps, at least one of these so-called adults was a snitch, a tattle tale... a "Karen".

The term "Karen" is a racist term. A simple online search reveals it describes the stereotypical white woman who complains, makes life miserable, and/or asks to speak to the manager. I don't approve of this term. It's not inclusive. After all, there are annoying women of all ethnicities, yet they have not been given a name. Until now! I propose we expand the category...

> Latina Karen = Karanita
>
> Asian Karen = Kai Ren
>
> Black Karen = KanayNay

As I said, working all week then driving to destinations on weekends wasn't cutting it. To see more of the world, I was going to have to transition into an alternative lifestyle. No, not become LGBTQ. Standup Comedy. *Tanx God* I made the leap. I'll never have to answer to losers about taking off my shoes ever again. (These days I answer to an entirely different set of morons.)

Today, I run my own company. No one looks over my shoulder (or under my desk). No one tells me how to get my work done. I'm the boss and I'm also the only employee. Our organization is proud to report we've had zero complaints of sexual harassment. (Technically, I harass my company's only employee every night before bed. Luckily, he keeps his mouth shut about it. Between me & me... *I think he likes it!*) This morning I ran for an hour, currently working from bed, and they can't stop me. I can't help but giggle, thinking of how upset the mystery coworker would be to find me writing this with no socks, no shoes, and if we're being completely honest, NO PANTS!

PACKING

Let's talk luggage. The friendly people at the airport flash a smile as they check your brand-new suitcase and place it on a conveyer belt. By the time you see it again, it appears as though it was hit by an IED in Fallujah. Dented, shredded, and zippers broken, yet nobody owns up to how or why this travesty happened. That's where Costco comes in handy. Their policy is: *"We take back anything at any time."* Therefore, I put that policy to work. I try to get two returns out of each suitcase before actually purchasing a new one. This means I'm still buying a suitcase every year or so, but at least I don't feel ripped off every time a wheel is.

Many airlines are charging for carry-on bags now. For small trips, get yourself a large backpack instead. You should be able to jam all the necessities in there for anything 3-days or less. If you can't = learn to pack better. A backpack is also great because it fits under the seat on the plane and you have access to it during a flight.

Low budget airlines are extra picky about what you bring on board since they love to upcharge whenever they can. One time I purchased a motorcycle in Texas and booked a cheap flight to pick it up. Would you believe they tried to charge me an extra $100 for my helmet?! "Sir, that counts as a carry-on." Thinking quickly, I PUT THE HELMET ON! (There's no rule against someone wanting to be *extra-safe* on a plane.) Everyone was looking at me like, "Um, does he know something about this flight that we don't?" I just wish I had a parachute to complete the outfit.

Headed to a wedding? You can still pack light. Consider wearing the tux on the flight to avoid the wrinkles that come with jamming it in a suitcase. You can change out of it as soon as you land. (I realize a bride might look a little ridiculous in her gown while sitting in 32B, but you may get bumped up to first-class... It's worth a shot!) What I'm saying is, there's always a way to make it work. Pack light and remember, they have stores wherever you're headed. You'll survive.

*TRAVEL HACK: BURNER CLOTHES

Combine your trip with some much-needed closet reduction. Take articles of clothing on their "last leg" and toss them out as you go. This lightens your load and leaves you more room for souvenirs. Plus, you'll return to a less cluttered home.

AIRPORT PICK UP/DROP OFF

Flex your travel expertise even before you get to the plane. In the early morning, it's best to get dropped off at the ARRIVALS area. Then take the escalator up to DEPARTURES.

In the evening, instead of getting picked up at ARRIVALS with hundreds of other frustrated drivers, simply go to DEPARTURES and instruct your ride to scoop you up there. By being a contrarian, you avoid being honked at, yelled at by pushy traffic cops, and jockeying for a place to load/unload.

CHAPTER 2: PLANES, TRAINS & THE TSA

Comedians spend so much time in airports that when we bring it up on stage, other comics roll their eyes. It's deemed "hacky" (meaning a topic that's already been hacked to death by all the other professionals). Crowds, on the other hand, can't seem to get enough of this type of material. So, hacky or not, we desperately try to find our own unique point of view on the topic and hack our way through.

I once had an airport experience that was not funny in the moment, but later proved to be great material.

While headed on a short trip, my dad suggested I take his little red duffle bag instead of my usual suitcase. I emptied it out, threw a few necessities inside and headed to the airport. Carry-on only, baby!

At the airport, I set it on the belt and waited for it to pass through the x-ray machine. The TSA agent looked extra close at his monitor – then suddenly called for backup. He then shouted to the others, "We got one!"

Two more agents hustled over to check the monitor.

I was excited because one of these travelers standing nearby must be a potential terrorist. Soon, I'd have a front row seat to watch them take down a bad guy. I tried to guess which one it was. None of them looked particularly "jihadi" to me. The TSA interrupted my investigation by pointing to me.

"IS THIS YOURS?!"

To my horror, *my bag* was lifted into the air. How could that be? Nothing was in it other than some clothes and a toothbrush... unless my underwear had set off a highly sensitive bomb threat. (Remind me to switch detergents.)

Three agents escorted me to a small room. They grilled me about the contents of my bag. I was clueless. They finally said "Look, we found this..." and that's when they pulled out a small bullet.

Suddenly it all made sense. This was my dad's old hunting bag. That little projectile had likely been wedged in there for years.

I explained all of this.

The TSA agent said that it was within their rights to now add me to a list for bringing artillery on a plane. That word felt a little excessive. *ARTILLERY?* They made it sound like I was packing a rocket launcher and missiles. This was just a lonely bullet. A bullet, mind you, *with no gun*! What was my grand plan – *threaten to throw it at people?!*

"Alright, EVERYBODY – Listen up. I have a bullet here. YES, IT'S REAL. I want my own row, and nobody is getting off this plane unless I get some more orange juice. THE WHOLE CAN. Do you hear me?!"

The TSA agents held a pow-wow and decided they could let me off with a warning, under one condition; that it NEVER HAPPENS AGAIN. I'd dodged a bullet.

Then I got even more nervous. Technically, now all anyone has to do is slip a small bullet in one of my bags and off to prison I go. I've wasted my one and only warning.

This is a totally true story. I've shared it many times on stage and received big laughs. After one show however, I was confronted by an irate comedian. "That's my joke! You stole it from me."

"Huh? How could I possibly steal it – when it *ACTUALLY HAPPENED* to me?"

"Because I went through TSA and they took my tweezers. So, I been saying, "What was I gonna do, tweeze people to death?"

In the mind of this idiot, it was beyond the realm of possibility that BOTH OF US might have had something confiscated by the TSA and arrived at a similar joke. (This is the level of intelligence you often deal with when working with comedians. A hazard of the job.)

I don't even tell the joke anymore and he's on his 23rd year of doing it (with no signs of stopping). As far as I'm concerned, he can have it. He may be *The Tweezerman*, but we all know who the real *BULLET BOY* is!

If he wasn't such a hater we could have paired up like tweezers and come together to form a dynamic duo, taking over the world with our weapons of mass destruction. But he didn't, so PLUCK HIM!

TSA

Ever seen our "Boys & Girls in Blueberry" and thought, "This is our last line of defense?" Do they look ready to *spring* into action? Luckily things rarely happen at an airport. There's more violence on your average *Bingo Night* at a Senior Community Center, but still.

I shudder to think of the man hours wasted daily around the world due to a handful of extremists. How many people are forced to leave their home an extra hour early to make time for degrading pat-downs? How many flights are missed because the security line is too long? These are the lasting effects of terrorism that few people consider: never ending inconvenience and trillions of dollars in wasted global productivity each year.

To avoid any perception of discrimination – every man, woman, and child must unpack then re-pack, dress then undress, in that kabuki theater of a line. To add to the indignity, they "randomly select" people for further pat downs. How about a little more profiling? Pretty sure Christine and her two kids – Skylar and Piper – aren't about to pull a jihad on their flight to Aspen.

There's never been a terrorist named Tucker, and even if there were, he would have already changed it to *Al-Tucki BinTuckistan*. Just look for that guy!

Meanwhile, the disabled may be getting off a little too easy. Sure, they look all sweet and innocent, but ya never know. While they are confiscating my water bottle, this guy is rolling right on by. Is that really a wheelchair or a series of pipe bombs cleverly welded together? You can easily turn a walker into a bazooka. (Pretty sure I saw that on *McGyver* once.) What I'm saying is they need to inspect people that look pro-Taliban *AND* the handicapped much harder than the rest of us.

TSA is so disrespectful – rubbing you up and down without even getting to know you and buying you a drink first. They always say, "Just so you know, I'll be using the back of my hand." What's the difference? Front. Back. If you're going there, do it right. By the way, you can still get turned on with knuckles hitting private regions over the clothes (just ask any Mormon teenager).

They tell us TSA stands for **T**ravel **S**ecurity **A**dministration. But I know the real meaning: **T**ouch **S**ome **A**—.

The new x-ray machines are more invasive than ever. I once asked, "Exactly how much detail can you see on that monitor?" The agent shrugged, "They're pretty revealing. Most of the time we can tell whether it's a man or a woman."

I thought about that for a moment, *"Most of the time?"* Which means, some of the time they can't. I'd hate to fall under the *UNSURE* category.

"Hmm, this one's a tossup. What do you think Janet? Ding-aling or AAA battery?"

Some of those TSA babes are cute. I want them to be so impressed with what they see on screen, they *request* a random pat-down and ask me what I'm doing later. So far, hasn't happened. Hope I'm not showing up as a "question mark".

If they're going to x-ray all of our belongings, why not let us lie down on the belt and go right through with our luggage. This way we can skip a visit to the doctor. Kill two birds with one stone. I want to know what's going on with my hip. Charge $100 for the service. I bet a few thousand people per day would take advantage of airport imaging services. We're talking millions in revenue per month and a much healthier society!

---

*TRAVEL HACK: SO THIRSTY

You aren't allowed to bring a bottle of water through security, but you *can* bring an empty one. Simply fill it up on the other side and save about $5 per flight.

OWN ROW

Anyone who follows me online will vouch for this, I often get my own row on flights. I love having three seats to myself, or as I call it, "Ghetto 1st Class."

A full row is actually better than most 1st class seats since you can lift the arm rests and lay flat. I had my own row to Hawaii once on a plane that had the 5 seats across the middle. Sure, the people in Business Class had a nice reclining chair, but I was completely stretched out. I had my laptop on one-side, my food and beverages on the other. At one point I woke up and did some yoga. I was actually a bit disappointed when we finally landed in Honolulu.

You may wonder how I get my own row so often while you are always crammed in a middle seat. Here are some tips (even though I should probably keep these a secret):

1. **PRIORITY:**
   Try to fly the same airline often so you have priority and can ask for an empty area of the plane.

2. **1st FLIGHT OUT:**
   Who the heck wants to wake up at 4am and head to the airport? YOU, that's who! Always opt for the 1st flight out. People miss early flights, which leaves more empty seats. Side benefit: the early flights are cheaper, there's no traffic on the way to the airport, the security lines are shorter, and the plane is already waiting for you. This means it is more likely to be on time. As they say, the early bird gets to lie down like a worm.

3. **BACK OF THE BUS:**
   Sit near the back of the plane. Passengers always congregate toward the front. How much time do they actually think they're saving? They still have to wait for their baggage. Plus, if the plane goes down they're gonna be the first to go!

SURGICAL MASK

Long before COVID, I was one of the only people that wore a mask on planes. It made me look contagious and guaranteed my own row on many Southwest Airlines flights where you pick your own seat. I came up with this idea after seeing an Asian guy wearing a mask on the plane back in 2012. Right then and there, I started doing it also.

(Copying off of Asians is a great idea and a key factor as to how I got into college. Always remember: Sit between two Wongs and you'll get everything RIGHT!)

*TRAVEL HACK: NOT WEARING A MASK

We live in a time where you may be forced to wear a mask on the plane. If these rules kick in again, slowly eat your pretzels, sip on a drink, or tie a bandana around your head just above your eyes and let it droop over your face. Now they don't know what you're doing under there.

RUDE PASSENGERS

One problem we all deal with – *rude travelers*. Sometimes it is their inexperience. Other times they should know better. Frustrations comes in many forms. Here are the most common offenders:

BEEPER KEEPER

This guy constantly beeps going through the metal detector but only removes one item at a time.

He realizes his watch is on. BEEP

It's the cell phone. BEEP
"Oh yea, my belt." BEEP

"Ahh, you think it's my satchel of lucky coins?"

Dude just get into your underwear and walk through like the rest of us, we're freezing back here!

CRY BABY

A wailing toddler is a tough one. Obviously, babies cry. But if your little mutant is screaming bloody murder and I look over to see you catching some ZZZ's we're gonna have a problem. Bounce him on your knee, jingle your keys, play peek-a-boo. TRY SOMETHING, FOR THE LOVE!

After 2 hours of "screaming baby" on one flight, I couldn't even blame the kid anymore. The parent needed to be reported to child protective services. I just started bellowing, "BAD MOM!" over and over again like *Rain Man.*

Since new age parents do the whole "we let our kid cry it out" routine, I came up with an even better invention. *The Bose Noise Canceling Baby Helmet.*

Kids are always wearing helmets, why not one for travel? Tell them they're Buzz Lightyear. The prototype I have in mind is especially cool with a drop-down screen for cartoons, speakers that play soothing tunes, a detachable mobile to watch things dance around above, and best of all – SOUND PROOF.

You can still see through the glass for wellness checks, but the rest of us don't have to hear a thing. (Come to think of it, this should also come in adult sizes.) The best part, it's already been tested on animals and works just fine.

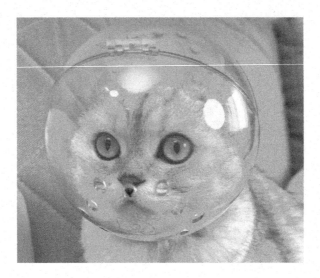

If interested, I'm looking for someone to help fund my idea. Act now before I take it to *Shark Tank*.

*Suggested retail price for the Noise Canceling Baby Helmet = $3,000 and worth every penny.

THE PLANE JUST LANDED

As soon as we land, morons from row 40 tend to think they have a shot at being the first ones off the plane – and by golly – they're going for it. They get to about row 37 before coming to a screeching halt, and now we're all crammed into an even tighter space than before.

Listen, get your rear-end back to your original seat, and let's get off this thing in a single file line.

Once, I was in the aisle seat as a lady came barreling toward the exit. I stuck my knee out and she plowed right into it.

"Excuse me sir, can you move your knee?"

"No"

"Sir, I'm getting off the plane."

"We're ALL getting off the plane. This isn't a bus. This is EVERYBODY'S STOP."

Some people avoid conflict. I lean into it. We were at a stalemate. She tried to get others on her side,

"Wow, this guy is offensive..."

Her crotch was about eye level, so I blurted out,

"You *smell* offensive."

I thought that was a pretty good one. Had this been a comedy club, it would have *killed*. However, on the plane, I got nothin'.

BAGGAGE

Everyone's got baggage (and no, I'm not talking about your ex). The question is, why doesn't anyone know how to collect theirs at the airport? The same person shoving you out of the way to get off the plane is now hovering over the carousel waiting 15 minutes for the luggage to drop.

If everyone would take two giant steps back, we could all walk up, collect what's ours as it comes around, and depart like civilized beings. No such luck!

Instead, I have to stare at a herd of backsides like animals at a watering hole in the Serengeti. When I finally see what perhaps *might* be my bag, it takes a running leap to get up and over the pile like a quarterback at the one-yard line. I wedge myself between an entire family, grab my suitcase, and fling it clear of the conveyer belt, taking out a grandpa in the process. He's now taken a Samsonite to the chin and he's down for the count!

*TRAVEL HACK: BAGS FLY FREE

Want to send 2 bags free to any town in the USA? Here's what you do: Buy a fully refundable 1st Class flight. Check your bags. Then 20 mins prior to departure, cancel for a full refund. It's too late for them to pull your bags off the plane. They'll now go to the destination as planned, FREE of charge, saving you hundreds in shipping fees!

PILOT SPEAK

When the pilot gets on the intercom more than once, it's typically to stutter and stumble through delivering some bad news. "…Uhhhh, this is your captain speaking. We uh, have discovered a uh, maintenance issue… We just uhhh wanted to let you know that uhhhhh we will update you as soon as we uhh have some more information from our uhh, ground crew. Thank you for your patience."

Can we stop with the pilot "Uhs?" Figure out what you're going to say before you get on the mic.

Could you imagine if your doctor spoke like that after running your blood work? "Uhhhh, we uh, need to take a uhh, another look at uhhh...."

You would cry out, "Give it to me straight doc! How long do I got left?"

LORD SPEAKS TO ME

I'm not scared to fly unless the turbulence gets really out of hand. I once sat next to an elderly woman that wasn't even the slightest bit concerned.

"Don't you worry. Nothin' bad is gonna happen on this flight."

"And how do you know?"

"The good Lord speaks to me."

"Is that so?"

"Oh yes, the other day I was at a coffee shop and the Lord said, 'You need to leave.' So, I did... And I'm glad I did."

"Why? What happened?"

"Well, how would I know? I left!"

Now that's what you call *FAITH*.

AIRPLANE MODE

I was on a plane once as the captain explained we were going to have a two-hour delay. Everyone groaned. Not me, I pulled out my phone to pass the time. That's when the flight attendant confronted me.

"Excuse me. Hi... Is that phone in 'Airplane Mode'?"

"Well, no but, we aren't going anywhere so..."

"Sir, this is still an active taxiway. You need to put that in 'Airplane Mode'. THANKS."

As she stormed off I muttered, "Why don't you put the *PLANE* in AIRPLANE MODE?!"

FLIGHT ATTENDANTS

Flight attendants are getting grouchier by the day, and they have every right to be. In the past they were young, hot women, happily inviting you to fly the friendly skies. Take a look at postcards from the 60's. Pan Am Airways hired nothing but pin-up models.

Pan American World Airways - Graduation 1962

Here we are, 60 years later, it appears some of these women ARE STILL FLIGHT ATTENDANTS! There's been no turnover in the industry. We went from *The Golden Age* of flying to *The Golden Girls* are flying.

Of course they're tired. Tired of the passengers, their feet hurt, and they lean so hard on that drink cart that it doubles as a walker.

They could care less about the safety announcement. They've done it ten thousand times while nobody even listens. Even if you happen to crash into the ocean and somehow survive, instinct will kick in and you'll simply cling to whatever is floating. You won't say, "Wait a minute, this isn't my seat cushion. This is a wing! I'm doing it all wrong. And where's that yellow life vest the lady kept telling me about for the past three decades?"

The effort they put into the safety announcement is so minimal they might as well not even do it. Often, they just play a video. When a flight attendant rattles it off, it just becomes one long run-on sentence. Try reading it as fast as they do:

Ladies and Gentleman: may I have your attention please...

WelcometotheBoeing737Aircraft, equipped with 2lavatories. 1inthefrontand1inthe back. Weaskthatyou put your seatbelt on and fasten it low andtightacross your hips, putyourtray tables in the uprightposotion, seatback forward,and prepare for takeoff. Intheunlikelyevent of a waterlanding the bottomofyourseat can beusedasa flotationdevice. IF the cabin loses pressureThe masks will come down. Put the strap over your head and breathe. Make sure you do yours firstbefore helpinganyothers. Wehave exits in the frontbackand overthewings. Notthatit much matters because ifwecrashwe're allgonnadieanyway. Now we ask that you sitbackrelax,

And THANK YOU for flying the Friendly skies.

As you can see, it's very hard to read all that and even harder to listen to. I have an innovative way to freshen up that stale safety announcement: flight attendants should merely WHISPER the whole thing into the microphone. When you yell at someone the listener retracts, but when a woman whispers she has your undivided attention!

At the very least it would make things a lot more interesting. Read this in your best Marilyn Monroe singing "Happy Birthday" voice and see for yourself:

"Hiii… thank you for getting on. Please put your seatbelt tight across your hips.

If you need more air, just pinch that thing above your head and give it a little twist.

Yea… just like that.

Oh, and if the mask comes down, strap it on. Make sure you do yourself first, then do your partner."

Riveting. Everyone is paying attention. Men's tray tables are already in the upright position. And nobody believes this is *Virgin Airlines*.

SKY DATING

Trying to land a date with a pretty flight attendant is almost impossible. We already discussed how rare they are. Now you must hope they're also single. A woman like that will not be on the market for long. Rest assured, they get hit on in all different ways by hundreds of passengers a day.

Then consider, you normally dress nice but on this flight you happen to be wearing tattered Batman pajamas. There goes your chance. Or what if you're in coach and she prefers to date First-Class?

All these things can work against you, but you should still shoot your shot. After all, let's say she's single. This means she's often away from friends and family, always in new towns, extremely bored, and looking for something to do. The airline pays for her hotels (which can be very lonely). Sure, pilots may hit on her, but they're all married. This is your chance to make the most of her *lay-over*.

Taking all this into account, I once flirted my way onto a date with a stewardess and it was glorious.

Half asleep, I noticed a great pair of legs walking up the aisle. I shook my head in disbelief. Perhaps this was just a dream. The second time she walked by, I was more alert. By the third time I was wide-awake for the rest of the flight.

The good news, by law, she would have to make that trip at least 13 more times. There would be plenty of chances to get her attention.

I had my own row but repositioned myself to the aisle. Thankfully I wouldn't have to talk over two other passengers as they rolled their eyes.

She was headed my way. No wedding ring. Things were looking good!

At 2 rows away, I could tell she was friendly, great smile, and gracefully handing out alcohol and peanuts. What's not to like?

As she moved closer I opened the window shade to shed more light on the situation. She was a brunette with highlights. She wore the uniform like it was made just for her. Those high heels were not regulation, but nobody was going to turn her in. One could say my tray table was headed into the upright position.

She finally got around to taking my drink order. Mustered up all my courage I said, "Orange juice, no ice, and your phone number on the napkin please."

Not bad, right? She laughed, which was good, then replied, "Wellll, I can definitely do the OJ." That wasn't great news, but if you examine her answer closely it was not a 'yes' or 'no'. I was still in the running, just needed to have good follow-up to nudge her in the right direction.

For my male readers, the key after using a cheesy pickup line is to be genuine from that point on. No need to keep dropping more dad jokes like, "How long you been a flight attendant? Cuz you been flying through my mind all day." Ew.

You'll look like you're trying way too hard with, "So, when are you and me gonna get UNITED?" Yuck!

Please never attempt, "You know, I also call my bedroom *The Cockpit.*"

Instead, I asked her where she was from, how she likes her job, and how many bags of peanuts she's allowed to give to one person. By the end of the flight I had earned her number.

There's supposed to be a three-day rule after getting the digits before calling to show you're not that eager. But who are we kidding, I was that eager! THIS IS A RULE TO IGNORE. Strike while the iron is hot. I decided to check-in right away with a quick text asking if she wanted to go for appetizers. She said, "Yes."

Within a few hours we were saying, "Cheers" over a glass of wine. SUCCESS. We had gone from 'airport strangers' to 'bottoms-up' in only a few hours. Before I knew it, clothes were ready for take-off and I was cleared for landing. Talk about 'Rapid Rewards'! She definitely had Spirit.

Best of all, she gave me a handful of "Buddy Passes" to fly FREE to any city I wanted. When they ran out, she gave me more. This sky babe was the gift that kept on giving.

Sadly, this story does end turbulently. Our relationship was just reaching a nice altitude when out of the clear blue sky, she told me it had to end. It turns out a pilot she worked with had swooped in and stolen her from me. I had not only lost the girl, but far more tragically, those valuable buddy passes as well. I asked if we could remain friends and would she be kind enough to continue sending them my way. She said, "Absolutely not." I couldn't believe she was clipping my wings so suddenly! "Why?" I snapped. "He's a pilot and already flies free. I'm the one who still needs them!" With that, she hung up and departed from my life as quickly as she'd arrived. It was a very quick turn-around and I've never heard from her since. It's as though she vanished into thin air. My eyes are getting a bit cloudy just thinking about it.

*TRAVEL HACK: ASK THEM TO BUMP YOU

If you have a little flexibility in your schedule, walk up to the gate agent and volunteer to get bumped *before* they have a chance to ask over the loudspeaker. This way you're already their top choice. By pre-emptively offering, I'm selected a few times a year. This has awarded me airport meals, free hotels and thousands of dollars in FREE FLIGHTS!

THERAPY DOG

There's been an increasing number of dogs wearing vests on planes. I think approximately 99% of these people are lying about their "condition". I could be wrong. It's probably closer to 99.9%, but it's illegal for businesses to question anyone. The mere idea of second guessing their need for the service dog makes you a villain up there with the likes of Hitler.

I'm not heartless. If you're blind, you absolutely deserve to have a dog accompany you. If you're a military vet with PTSD, you earned that four-legged friend – *Thank you for your service.*

But there's an abundance of able-bodied people with lap dogs. Ever ask them what the dog does for them? They always give the same answer, "Oh, Poofy is an emotional service animal. I'm scared to fly, and she recognizes when I'm having anxiety." Really? Then why is your dog shaking more than you are right now? Do y'all take turns or something?

I know one guy who has a service dog because – get this – HE HAS A STUTTER! Now, how the hell does the dog help with that? I mean, he does sound really stupid when he talks but there's not much the pooch can do about it.

*Unless it's trained to bite anyone that bullies him. What's the command? "Bu-Bu-Bu-Buh-Bite that G-g... ATTACK!"

A service dog should have actual skills, not just a jacket purchased on Amazon. Here's a quick guide so you can easily decipher if it's a real service animal or not.

PROBABLY A SERVICE ANIMAL...

GERMAN SHEPHARD

LABRADOR

GOLDEN RETRIEVER

MOST LIKELY FULL OF SHITZU...

EVERY OTHER DOG

Nobody ever trained a Chihuahua to do anything. Did you know they can't even say, "Yo Quiero Taco Bell"? We've been lied to!

I should take the opportunity to commend these liars for at least having a DOG. The reason you have to put your foot down early on stuff like this is because people push the limits. Give them an inch and they'll take a *mule*. Indeed, it might be too late. Due to our lenient standards, many are seeing just how far they can go with other types of so-called "Service Animals".

Recently, airlines cracked down on all this because obvious abuses were taking place. Travelers have shown up to the airport with therapy ducks, lizards, possums, gerbils, kangaroos... even a therapy horse was brought onto a plane. It was getting to be a real zoo up there.

As a comedian, people always think I'm just joking, but this is absolutely true. Don't believe me? Do an online search of all the animals they've had up there. I'll wait...

There's barely any legroom on a plane as it is. I don't want to share it with the cast of *Charlotte's Webb*. Old MacDonald had a farm, but DELTA is not its NAME-O.

And why is it always some form of therapy animal and not a plant? I've never seen a therapy orchid, or emotional support daffodils. Those things relieve stress, too. You've never seen one person on board who declares, "If you'll excuse me, I'm going to destress now and trim my Bonsai."

*TRAVEL HACK: GO "SEE" A MOVIE

Want to see a movie for free? Put a generic vest on your dog, don some sunglasses, and walk right on into the theater. Look straight ahead and blow right by the usher's podium. It's not illegal to wear sunglasses and walk into places with a dog. Most teenagers working the entrance will be too shy to stop you. If they try and get your attention pretend you also can't hear. If all else fails, stare into the distance and say, "I don't need a ticket, I'm not here to watch a movie." Then keep on walking. Let me know if it works.

LOST HIS ARMS

I love people who overcome disabilities. I read a story about a guy who lost his arms in a tragic accident but learned to type 80 words per minute using only his NOSE!

Problem was, none of the words made sense: qwerty, uiop, asdfgh... Things like that. Don't even ask me what words those are. Nobody NOSE but him!

SEEING EYE DOGS FOR THE BLIND

Growing up, my family volunteered for a program called *Seeing Eye Dogs for the Blind.* We'd get a Labrador puppy sent to our home every two years. Our job was to train them up-to-speed before they were paired with a blind person. The pooch could go to school with us, supermarkets, work... anywhere! They were simply puppies, but it was important to prepare them for the higher learning that was to come.

Sometimes store managers would try to kick us out of an establishment and we could give them a snarky reply and stand our ground, knowing the law was on our side.

The only downside, it was sad to have to give them back after bonding with these adorable puppies. But a new little bundle of joy would arrive a few weeks later.

With that said, I always had a passion for well-trained dogs. In fact, when I see an animal misbehave, I shake my head – *at the OWNER!* Sadly, comedians travel so much, having a dog or even a girlfriend is very hard. (I'm most upset about the dog.) Therefore, in 2019 – I made the decision to get RENO, an adorable Boxer.

Without the strict rules of the *Seeing Eye Dogs* program I could teach him all kinds of unorthodox tricks. He is so ugly he is cute. Or so cute he's ugly? Either way he provides countless hours of entertainment.

Once RENO was trained up to my standards, I *suddenly* developed a deep fear of planes. It was the darndest thing. My doctor wrote me a note, which allowed him to join me on flights all over the USA. He was so well behaved it never raised an eyebrow. Sadly, not everyone acted as responsibly. Some people brought dogs that bit airline staff. Then all those other exotic animals were brought onboard.

It made me mad they were abusing a program that I was abusing. What I did was *Regular Unethical*, but like a gas pump, those people are what I call *Super Unethical*. The nerve!

Because of that, all the airlines have now done away with Emotional Support dogs on planes. A fun loophole while it lasted, I must now take him to formal Service Dog training and develop a new illness. If you have any good ones, I'm currently taking suggestions.

WHO GETS THE DOG?

I was watching a TV program discussing who should get the dog in a divorce or breakup. This can create some of the biggest arguments at the end of a relationship. That's when I decided we should have couples sign a PrePuptual Agreement.

Gotta get a PrePup!

BANDANA BANDIT

The past few years I've worn a bandana when I travel. It's become one of the most important accessories I own for a variety of reasons. Allow me to demonstrate all the ways a scarf can enhance your travel experience...

1. **BLINDFOLD:**
   On the plane, if some idiot won't put their window shade down, simply blindfold yourself. Enjoy pitch-black sleeping conditions no matter where you sit.

2. **FASHIONISTA:**
   Ever have to speak with customer service? Simply tie the scarf around your neck and sachet up to the counter. With a few limp-wristed movements and a hint of a lisp, ask for whatever favor you're looking for. Customer service is much more likely to upgrade that rental car, put you in the first-class cabin, or give you a room with a view if they think you're a member of a protected minority group and accustomed to living a FABULOUS life.

3. **EARMUFFS:**
   A bandana can keep the winter air from blowing into your ears. 70% of your body heat dissipates through

your head, so keep yourself warm while your friends shiver, all because you were smart enough to reposition your bandana. If you have headphones on, the bandana keeps them pressed closer to your ears, giving you enhanced audio quality.

4. **50 SHADES OF K:**

   Let's say, hypothetically, you meet a beautiful flight attendant and want to use it on her... *just saying!*

5. **GANGSTAAA:**

   Find yourself in a questionable part of town? No problem! Spin that bandana around and show the homies you mean business. It'll intimidate people that might otherwise attempt to try you in a back alley. From a distance you look a little like Tupac and nobody wants to tangle with a guy who's living that THUG LIFE.

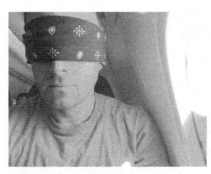

CHAPTER 3: HOTELS & RENTAL CARS

Rental cars are my absolute favorite. You can reserve them all over the world and don't even have to pick them up. There's no charge for failure to appear. I wish jury duty had that policy.

Something fun a guy can do: approach any attractive female working the counter and proclaim, "Hate to brag but I'm built like a rental car, you know why?" Then point down and say, "HERTZ!"

Once, on an unfamiliar freeway – a flash went off. I thought nothing of it but found a ticket waiting in the mail. It informed me I was going 8 miles over the speed limit and now owed $450. Then a letter from the rental car company arrived, stating they'd paid it with my card on file while adding a $250 convenience fee for the effort. Then my insurance went up $400 per year. All this bad luck, simply because the camera caught my license plate. I'm old fashioned, if the police want to make some money for the city and write me a ticket, fair enough, but none of this mailing photos and ruining my life. From that day forward I decided to bend my plates in half. That's right! (They're made of flimsy tin after all.) Each time I pick up a rental car, I simply fold the plate. They're still on the car and a human can read it, but a camera will have trouble making out the final two numbers. Game on. CATCH ME IF YOU CAN.

This trick works for running red lights as well. Not to mention bridges & tolls. For example, each time you enter San Francisco they scan your plate and you owe the city approximately $10. It costs $23 to go in and out of NYC during peak hours. Not me! I'm like a low budget Al Capone, bootlegging myself in and out of any town I want.

The cops are so overwhelmed, demoralized, and defunded that in 10 years of doing this, I've only been pulled over once for this stunt. The officer wanted to know why my plate was bent in half. I played dumb and asked him what he meant by that. He said, "Your plate, it's like... folded." I said, "Sir, this is a rental car. You're not making any sense. Can I get out and see what you mean?" He agreed, and together we went to the back of the car to inspect my plate. I feigned outrage. "How embarrassing. This is the worst rental car company ever!" I kicked the bumper for dramatic effect. "First they promised me an upgrade, and now this?!"

He asked me to please calm down. I then bent the plate back to normal while uttering a few more choice words about the company burdening me with this subpar vehicle. He felt bad and told me there's nothing to worry about anymore. I'm sure he wanted to write me a fix-it ticket but I'd just fixed it, so he had no choice but to send me on my way.

2 MONEY SAVING RENTAL CAR TIPS:

1. **Insurance:**
   Check with your car insurance & credit card company, you may already be double covered for a rental car. No need to purchase their extra insurance no matter how hard they pressure you.

2. **Refueling:**
   When returning your car, refuel about 40 mins away from the airport. The gauge will still read FULL, but you were able to squeeze $10 worth of fuel out of it.

*TRAVEL HACK: MOBILE OFFICE

Need a quiet place to work on your laptop, conduct a conference call, or take a nap? Go to the rental lot of any major airport and sit in any car you choose. These cars are always unlocked with the keys inside. As long as you don't attempt to drive off the lot, it's yours for a few hours. If an employee approaches, tell him you're about to get going but don't want to text and drive. That should buy you another 20 minutes. Then inform them you're a GOLD MEMBER and would like to know their badge number. They'll leave you alone for the rest of the afternoon. (Especially if you're wearing your bandana as a decorative scarf.)

SORTIE

While making my way through Europe, I connected with a buddy of mine. He'd conjured up an itinerary that was insane. It was packed with things like, "We must catch this train so we can do lunch in Milan... then be on this one in order to arrive in Florence for dinner." This continued for 9 days. We departed Italy on a train headed for the beautiful coastal town of Nice. Once we crossed into France, I was not familiar with the new language. We pulled into a train station and I noticed SORTIE written on the pillars. These were the days before smartphones, so I'm looking on various maps to chart our course and concluded we had somehow made a wrong turn.

Our intended stop was Nic Riquier or Nice Saint-Augustin, not Sortie?! I showed my friend that Sortie wasn't even one of the options and yelled at him, "Get off now. We're on the wrong train. We're gonna miss the sunset in NICE!"

I threw him his bag and we jumped onto the platform. Running to the stairs he paused, "Wait a minute. This *stop* isn't Sortie. SORTIE means EXIT in French, YOU IDIOT!"

Oh, NO! Back on the train, back on the train. The doors were closing as I slipped aboard the same car we'd just gotten off. It was pulling out. I looked back to see my buddy getting jammed by the door multiple times as he tried to squeeze through with his large backpack. I forced the doors open as he spilled into the train. The French just looked at us over their newspapers exactly like you might expect.

I'm just glad we got that all *sortied* out before it was too late.

*MONEY SAVING TIP:

Find a book on *how to save money*, but don't buy it — simply thumb through it right there in the bookstore. Boom! I just saved you $18. Don't worry, the author will appreciate how committed you are to his principles.

SUBWAY

Riding a NY subway is always an adventure. These cars are sterilized roughly every decade or so. Some passengers tap away on their phones, while others perform, sleep, or brawl. The homeless will use the subway as an ATM working their way down the aisles begging for cash. There's never a shortage of characters getting on and off.

My last train ride, I found myself people-watching with the hopes that some of this might inspire some comedy bits. As the train rumbled down the track and my mind began to wander, I was interrupted by a man directly across from me clearing his throat. I glanced up and he suggested with a nod that I look to my right.

To my horror, a yellow puddle was ever-so-slowly creeping its way directly toward me. The homeless guy laying across the seats next to mine had passed out and decided that getting up to use the restroom was too much of an inconvenience.

Disgusted, I jumped up and moved one seat over. Ahhh, much better. I was safe for now as the pee was four feet away instead of one. *New York logic.*

While I was happy to get a warning from my fellow passenger, I do not feel it was the appropriate level of concern. Let it be known that if you notice hobo fluids coming my way, don't casually nod and hint vaguely! I need you to stand up like a hero in an action film, grab me by the arm and fling me to safety. I need to be halfway ready to fight you. Then notice urine and collapse back into your arms in appreciation. Chivalry is officially dead in NYC.

---

*MONEY SAVING TIP:

Gentleman's clubs are expensive. Save cash by asking to audit a local pole fitness class to see if it's something you'd be into. Not only is it free, they highly discourage tipping!

HOTELS

Stay at the Ritz Carlton for $1,800 a night and they charge you to park, eat breakfast, use the resort, get a cocktail, and do laundry. Stay at a $59 roadside motor lodge and they throw all that in for free (plus give you a delicious cookie at check-in). It makes no sense!

As you know, I often take the 5am flight. Hotel breakfast lasts from 6-9am. That means I rarely get to enjoy this perk. One time I left a hotel, landed in a new town, and saw the same chain right by the airport. In my humble opinion, they still owed me brunch. So, I walked in and made myself a plate. (I still had my room key in case an employee asked.)

That's the moment I realized no matter how bad things got, I'd never starve. Simply look presentable, walk into any mid-level hotel like you belong there, grab some food, eat, and leave. You could work your way around the country for a decade and never hit the same location twice. Imagine actually gaining weight as a vagabond all thanks to The Vagabond. What about a shower, you ask? The hotel pool awaits!

The most important thing is to save money on lodging. After all, you're only sleeping there. Hotel prices fluctuate a lot. Lock-in the best one you can find a month before your trip. Make sure it offers Free Cancellation. Then double-check the price about 1 week out to see if you can beat it. You don't want to be paying $230 a night for something that is now going for $130. When booking a hotel, I also look for 3 things:

- *Free Parking*
- *Free Breakfast*
- *No Resort Fees*

One time I was able to snag an amazing deal on a hotel in San Francisco at $70 a night, only to find parking was $75. My car was out there costing me more than I was. If only there was a way to bring it into the room!

*TRAVEL HACK: HALVE YOUR PARKING PASS

If a guest comes to visit you at the hotel, why pay two full parking fees? Simply cut your parking pass in half and jam them in the windshield by the dashboard. The hotel security is looking for vehicles with no association to the hotel. They won't tow if, with a quick inspection, they see your pass proudly displayed. Now you've parked two for the price of one!

CHAPTER 4:
DIS-ORIENTED IN ASIA

An email from Nobel Prize Laureate Dr. Muhammad Yunus appeared, inviting me to perform in Thailand. My first thought, was this that Nigerian Prince again?! He's fooled me a few times in the past.

After some investigation, it turned out to be legit. The inventor of micro-lending had stumbled upon my first book *Once You Go Persian* and decided his philanthropic business conference needed some comic relief.

I knew of him already because he'd appeared with U2's Bono and recently received the Congressional Medal of Honor from Barack Obama. I accepted the invite, booked my flight, and started thinking of some ideas of my own for his big event.

Recently single, I couldn't wait to bring laughs to Thailand, enjoy the food, and of course meet exotic Thai women. I was warned by a good friend, "Beware. In that region, some objects are not as they appear."

Unsure what he meant, it was then spelled out for me,

"Some of the women in Thailand, *ARE NOT WOMEN.*"

I laughed it off, "Ohh. Yea, but you can tell."

"NAHHH, DUDE. YOU CAN'T TELL..."

By the sound of his voice, I could tell he had been tricked.

After some research I learned Thailand is the gender change capital of the world, and over the past few decades the medical community has really excelled in the practice.

To get more insight I asked a local how one might spot the difference. His words haunt me to this day. In a thick Thai accent, he declared "If dey are very pret-tee. Very verrry beau-tee-foo. Dat's lady-boy!"

Very beautiful? Very pretty? That changed everything. I walked into a few bars and walked right back out. There were way too many hot chicks in there. NO THANKS.

I know that may sound a bit intolerant, but I'm old fashioned. That is merely my preference. I don't want an fruit-in-those-looms. And I don't want to be shamed about it either. I like my women the way progressives like their salad: Organic, Non-Genetically Modified, Hormone-Free... *and I'm allergic to nuts.*

Sure, I was going to Thailand, but I wasn't going to "Bang-Kok". The time had come for the conference and I was able to make a large global audience laugh. Important people always seem to present Dr. Yunus with elaborate gifts or awards when they meet him, and I didn't want to leave him empty handed.

To his surprise, I'd modified one of my *Once You Go Persian* t-shirts into his signature look, complete with wood buttons. I presented it to him as a gift on stage and the audience roared with approval. He was a good sport and kept it on for the rest of the evening.

THAI MASSAGE

Thailand is known for their massages. I saw one location called Koon Massage and thought that was very funny. In Thai, "Koon" is a title that bestows respect. However, in my Persian culture, "Koon" translates to "butt". Therefore, the title had a double meaning and I couldn't help myself. I posted a video, "Look, they only massage 'koons' here. That's their specialty!" All my Iranian fans were delighted, joking in the comments section. Many said they sure could go for a koon massage themselves.

We had a great time with never-ending bun puns. That is until one commenter wrote, "Wow, y'all just openly racist against us black folk, huh? I'm gonna report each and every one of you for these comments."

What was he even talking about? One-by-one we started getting banned from the social media page and locked out with a warning for "violating community standards".

Then it hit me. This little activist didn't realize "koon" was a fun Persian word. To him, it could only mean one thing: a derogatory name for black people. He had focused on a *THIRD* definition and thought we were all laughing about African-Americans. This was the furthest thing from our minds. It was clear, the massage parlor's funny name had really become a pain in my @$$!

A few commentors tried explaining the translation to him, but he was not having it. From his point of view, he'd uncovered a great racial injustice and could not be persuaded otherwise.

This is one of the clearest examples I have of someone being offended before knowing the whole story and blowing their koon out of proportion.

Remember, the world is a big place. Before you get upset or think you are a victim, perhaps there's another explanation. These are just some of the deep thoughts I'm having while simultaneously enjoying a deep koon massage right now.

NOT THAT KIND OF MASSAGE

While in Bangkok, I was encouraged to try an authentic Thai massage, but to be cautious. Locations that do their business upstairs were not very "reputable".

I strictly wanted a massage. No funny business. Yet, each massage parlor I approached turned out to just be a door that led up a flight of stairs to the mysterious second floor. I was getting discouraged.

Finally, I peeked in a window and was pleased to find a row of massage tables right there on the first floor. Eureka! I walked in and was told they could see me right away. I paid and the lady gestured for me to follow her. That's when we walked right past the beds... and UPSTAIRS!

What the?! Upstairs? That's what I'd been TRYING to avoid. She opened the door to a private room with bare walls and a large mattress on the floor. (I'd lived in a fraternity house and was quite familiar with this décor.)

Uneasy about now being upstairs in a Thai massage parlor I decided to go with it, but told myself if anything came up to make it very clear I was here for MASSAGE ONLY.

My masseuse handed me cotton pants and a shirt and said she'd be right back. Now in America, we just wear our underwear during bodywork and I wanted the best pressure possible, so I wasn't about to put on a t-shirt and capris.

Opting to leave them to the side, I disrobed down to my boxers, slipped under the top sheet, and waited. The lady walked back in and was shocked to see I hadn't put on the clothing. She nervously giggled and chastised me in a beautiful Thai accent,

"NO, NO... YOU PUT PANT ON."

"But, my boxers are on..."

"I sorry. We not that kind of place. We do massage only here!"

"What? I want massage only!"

"No, no. You bad boy! Put pant on. Then we do just massage!"

Wait, now *I* was the bad boy? No. *She* was the bad girl. I didn't even want to be up here in the first place! *I* wanted to be on full display for the whole city. Downstairs. In front of the window.

We got it all worked out and then it became clear why it was so important to wear the little karate outfit. Thai massage is unlike any other. They don't just rub your back. Through the course of the massage, this woman sat on top of me. Flipped me over. Put me in a chokehold. Arched my back. Pushed my legs over my head. Stepped on my crotch while pulling on my ankle. At one point she tagged out and her partner jumped in off the top ropes. I didn't know this was going to turn into a WWE event.

It made perfect sense why she was offended. I can't imagine trying to do all of those acrobatics in my tattered boxers. They would have never survived the ordeal. Plus, all that rolling around with two women, they would have eventually said, "I knew it. YOU BAD BOY!"

*TRAVEL HACK: FREE WATER AT EVERY HOTEL

Bottled water can cost big bucks in your room. Instead, head to the fitness center where they have the best filtered/bottled water for free. I've also seen apples & oranges at times. While you're down there, do a quick mile on the treadmill.

A HANDY THING TO HAVE IN SINGAPORE

Speaking of lost in translation, I arrived in Singapore and the hotel was one of the nicest I'd seen. The lady at the front desk told me about all the different amenities that were included with the hotel and I was blown away. Then she revealed one of their newest offerings: I would be getting a handy once I got to my room.

"Excuse me?"

"As a thank you for staying with us you will get a handy."

"Really!?"

"Yes, we realize when you travel, this might be something you need to make your stay more enjoyable."

This was some world-class service!

I slowly walked to my room. Nobody followed. I opened the door and called out with a timid "Hello...?", but nobody was there.

I waited for 20 minutes, but still no handy. Maybe they forgot which room I was in. I went to call front desk and that's when I realized, a "Handy" is what they call a smart phone.

Each room has one that you can take around town during your stay. A very nice feature, just not what I expected. I grabbed it and went off to explore the city, and that was the only thing that came in handy that day.

NASTY LAMA

In Malaysia I was excited to try the local fare for the first time. There was a vendor in a park and he proudly displayed a row of banana leaves folded like little presents. Several people came up and grabbed one. They were going for $2, so I got in on the action.

After the purchase, which is never the right order, I asked, "Hey, what is this anyway?"

"You must try. Nasty lama..."

"Ok, but like what is it?"

"Is nasty lama."

"Oh, ok, that makes more sense."

Their plan – keep repeating the same thing until the stupid American eventually understood Malay. Kinda wishing I had a handy right about now.

I sat down at a picnic table and opened the banana leaf like a kid on Christmas day.

Once undone, to my horror, a dry shriveled fish head plopped out. It had been resting on a ball of white rice with a red sauce on it. I reminded myself that I asked for this.

Avoiding the dead fish, I poked the brownish-red paste with my finger and gave it a taste. Turns out it is an incredibly hot sauce that sticks around. It spread throughout my mouth. I quickly ate some rice but that didn't stop the sensation. The fish head would now be my only salvation. I learned a valuable lesson – If someone tells you their food is *nasty anything...* believe them.

Addendum: After four days in Malaysia I've been eating *Nasi Lemak* regularly. You absolutely must try it!

*TRAVEL HACK: IS THERE A DOCTOR IN THE HOUSE?

When signing up for a credit card, the drop-down menu asks you to specify Mr, Mrs, or Dr. It's not illegal to pretend you're a doctor. Select it and watch how much more respect you get wherever you go. Once they see your card, FREE UPGRADES await for the good doctor!

KOREAN KIT KAT

Seoul is simply amazing. You can walk for hours and see no litter on the streets. The people come from a variety of economic backgrounds but there are no makeshift shelters or tent cities under any overpass.

A beautiful river runs through the middle of downtown with stones set along the way which allow for midstream crossing. I walked it at night and marveled at the lights illuminating the way.

It occurred to me that in the USA, this would not be a safe place to be at night. A small minority of vagrants, hobos, and questionable characters would have claimed this area and taken the opportunity away from the citizens to enjoy.

I made my way high atop a hill to a lookout point. You think the skyscrapers of New York are impressive? They got nothing on this place. With 10 times the population, it's like a full Manhattan skyline, but in every single direction. 360 degrees.

Making my way back downtown I looked up and chuckled. For some reason the Koreans had decided the Kit Kat candy bar, the ones we throw at kids on Halloween, was a delicacy deserving of its own restaurant.

There was a huge line for the chocolate covered wafer we take for granted. I had to see what all the fuss was about. Once inside it was clear they took this very seriously. You didn't just order a Kit Kat and walk out; you were treated to an experience.

They hand you a menu and you decide, would you like your Kit Kat decorated with nuts and drizzled with caramel? How about laced with bacon and spices?

What was going on here? I settled for the Kit Kat fruit parfait. They brought it out as if they were presenting a Michelin rated platter.

Admittedly it was good, but this was a little too much fanfare. Once the bill arrived, I had changed my mind. $35 for a Kit Kat? *Give me a break!* That was the first and last time I'll ever be enjoying that "elegance" at a sit-down establishment.

*TRAVEL HACK: TIP YOUR HOTEL MAID

Always leave your maid a tip. It's good karma. Plus, if you accidentally leave something behind, they're a bit more inclined to return it. It seems, if you don't take care of the housekeeper, they can never seem to locate your shoe, charger, or laptop.

PERSIAN FOOD

A lot of my fans are from Iran. After comedy shows we often find ourselves deciding where to eat in celebration of a great night.

But here's a little secret about Persians – they only want to eat PERSIAN FOOD. Sure, they just had it last night, and they're having it tomorrow, but they want it *NOW*. You could suggest Chinese, Japanese, Indian, Cuban, Colombian, Hawaiian, Jamaican… One by one they will shoot them all down. While I love Persian food, I also like variety.

I plead, "What about Thai?"

"Actually, there is dis great Persian place right next to Thai restaurant."

"Okay, Asian Fusion."

"Vhy not Persian Fusion?"

They then say something sneaky,

"Let's not argue. We vant to be fair. So ve take a vote."

Then all six Persians vote "Persian" while you are the lone vote for anything else.

"That settles it... Persian it is!"

One night I'd had enough. I was in Ottawa for the evening and had already enjoyed Persian food 43 nights in a row. I told the whole group of new friends that I'd just met I would be having Vietnamese if anyone wanted to join me.

They tried to persuade me that there is a Persian restaurant owned by a wonderful Vietnamese lady on the other side of town, but I wasn't having it. I stood firm, VIETNAMESE.

They all looked at each other and shrugged, "Ok. Ok, ve go."

We went to a restaurant with a great vibe. They had a huge menu. I ordered the Vietnamese soup. It was delicious, but hard to enjoy because across the table sat a row of Persians looking down at their plates like they were being poisoned. The faces they made to each other, the forced conversation as they nudged one another under the table. They kept switching to Farsi so I wouldn't be able to understand what they were saying, but it was fairly obvious. They were trying to organize another meal after this at a Persian restaurant to cleanse their pallet.

From now on, I just go wherever they want. It isn't worth all the shade that comes along with going somewhere *other than* Persian. And since they're Persian, they offer to pay, and I GLADLY LET THEM!

GOOD PHO YOU

I love Vietnamese soup (aka Pho). As a comedian, telling jokes and mingling nightly with fans can take a toll on the throat.

If you catch a cold or feel something coming on, nothing beats a big bowl of broth filled with fresh ingredients, vegetables, and lime.

I've tried pho all around the world and one thing you have to respect is how creative they get with the restaurant names. I was at one called *Good Pho You*. I found myself smiling while eating my soup thinking, "Yea, this is good pho me!"

In Las Vegas there's a popular Vietnamese place owned by a woman named Kim Long. It's open 24-hours and she named it after herself. So, it's *Pho Kim Long*.

Say that three times fast. She wants people to enjoy pho whenever. Pho Kim Long, all day/all night. That's a name that really works for Sin City.

At that moment I came up with my own idea for a Vietnamese restaurant with drive-thru only. Name it "GO PHO YOURSELF!" (We're currently looking for investors.)

If you don't like it – *pho you!* You can go somewhere else. I envision them like Starbucks with one on every corner. It's bound to be a hit with merchandising alone.

*Another business idea: I want to open my own place that makes the best folded French pastries. I'm calling it, "I'm Tired of Your CREPE!"

PHO BOMB

When a steaming hot bowl of Pho comes out, it's fun to add your own sauces. One afternoon, I decided to test my limits and go "extra spicy". Shoveling in chili flakes was just the start, I then added Sriracha hot sauce, and topped it all off with two scoops of dark red chili paste. This wasn't going to be soup; this was going to be a test of my manhood!

Plunging that big plastic spoon into the bowl, I braced myself for the concoction. As I leaned in for that first bite, I became a victim to the following chain of events:

- A large hunk of broccoli decided to go rogue.
- The bulbous vegetable dove off the spoon and into the soup below.
- It hit the nuclear concoction I'd created with a great plop.
- That splash came right back up and into my eyes.

Now, I had the hottest soup ever created directly in both eyeballs. At that moment, the Asian server walked by to check on me, "How's your soup?" I looked up at her squinting but trying to fight through the pain, nodding, "Oh, very good."

She gave me a funny look.

From her point of view, I appeared to be mocking her in a very racist fashion. Just what she needed, an arrogant American doing a bad Asian impersonation to her face.

"Very good. Ow. Thank youuu!"

We never spoke after that. With tears streaming down my face I felt even worse due to the misunderstanding and left her an extra tip.

Hope she reads this and realizes, "He wasn't racist guy. He just had pho in eye."

FOOD IS THE KEY TO LOVE

People always ask me, "K-von what's the secret to winning the heart of a gorgeous woman?" So, I wrote this poem. Pay attention guys...

THE SECRET TO KEEP HER

You've got to keep her well fed, from morning 'til bed
Whip out that spread. Make her eat bread
On your first date, make her put on that weight
Load her up like a train, until she's carrying freight

Give her Thanksgiving for breakfast, tell her gravy is groovy
Hide lard in that smoothie while she's watching a movie
If she thinks she's gettin' big, tell her, "No way, you're ok!"
Then before she hits the hay, take her to a buffet

She'll be working out hard, but it'll be too late
She'll be clogging her heart, and she'll keep gaining weight
And she'll be stuck on you, and she'll be stuck like glue
She'll be stuffed like a turkey, wonderin' how she done grew

Pull up to the ice cream man, tell him you're his biggest fan
Give him all your money, then take off in his van
Make her load up on sauce, this way your girl don't take off
Tell her, "Yes it's lactose free" and then just stuff it with cheese

You got to show her you love her, smother her broccoli with butter
Make sure she's flattered. Make sure all her food's battered
Her friends may say she's getting fatter, tell her "Forget all that chatter!"

Your love deserves some hors d' oeuvres, you should be ready to serve
Into the drive-through is where your car needs to swerve
Order fried chicken, and churros, and cherry cream pies
Get her chalupas, and chocolates… be sure to upsize

If you know what's up, you gotta 'Grande' that cup
Got to protect what's yours, you got to fatten her up
She'll try to take charge again, when she sees she's enlargin'
Take healthy food mislabel the jars it's in, so she's eating margarin

Other dudes be like, "Damn dog, look at her size"
But at the end of the day you'll be grabbing those thighs
Tell her you won't be home, until you can't see her bones
Then order some pizzas my partner, pick up the phone

You need to squirt catchup, all up on her potatoes
When she's not looking, you got to slap on the mayo
You can be relieved when she's too big to leave
Get your girl eating gluten more than 8 days a week

Tell her you don't like her rump, unless it starts to get plump
Tell her you won't be her hubby, until she starts to get chubby
The day that you marry her, take a good look at her derrière
Cuz, by the time she dies it's gonna take a dump truck to bury her

Pour some cream in her coffee, then sprinkle with toffee
Bring her muffins in bed (I'm talkin' blueberry & poppy)
Have her sample all the different forms of ham that you're making
Force feed her 6 degrees of pork, as if her name's Kevin Bacon

Tell your mom, "Cook her food, be like Nike, JUST DO IT"
Tell your girl she's being rude if she refuses to chew it
Safely call her your sweetie after she gets diabetes
Now she's a Perfect 10, so jab her with an insulin pen

Tell her she looks best when she fills out that dress
And that's the secret to keep her… you just have to feed her!

CHAPTER 5: MOMS WHO FLOAT

One of my most memorable standup comedy performances took place on a yacht in Newport Beach. It was Mother's Day weekend and I had the privilege of performing for 200 wealthy moms while tooling around on one of the most beautiful coasts in the world.

I was the only man allowed on board. The food was great. Plus, I knew if by chance the boat were to sink, all the Orange County moms would FLOAT! (Let's just say, many come equipped with their own *flotation devices*.)

They'd be in the bay waiting for help to arrive. They wouldn't even be sea-level, that's *D-Level*!

I told that joke during my performance and one mom complained after the show. "We wouldn't all float. Mine are natural." By looking at her lips, I could tell she was going to float differently.

The ones I was most concerned about were the younger OC ladies with the newer backside procedures. I call those the Kim KreditKardAssians. Based on the implant placement, they'd be floating #Suns-Out-Buns-Out.

BETTA' THAN SEINFELD

Speaking of Mother's Day, one year I performed on Long Island for a group of wealthy moms. The town was called Great Neck, so for my first joke I remarked that it was aptly named. After all, these ladies had some great necks!

The fun continued for an hour or so and I'll never forget a compliment I received on the way out from one of the mothers.

With a thick Lawn-Guyland accent she said, "I wanna tell ya. I suawww Jerry Sueiiiinfeld, and I enjoyed your show betta..."

I was humbled, "Oh come on, there's no way I'm funnier than Jerry Seinfeld."

She came right back with, "You weren't. But your show was cheapa' – Soooo, I ENJOYED IT BETTA."

At that point I was TRULY humbled.

SENSITIVE SWEDES

Based on my experience assembling IKEA furniture, I should have known dating a girl from Sweden would be difficult. (At least the furniture comes with vague instructions.)

I've dated women from around the world, but Hilda from Stockholm holds the record for the most emotionally sensitive ever encountered. She had just moved to the USA and I was the first American guy she'd gone out with.

With the average girl, you might say, "Hey, come with me, let's go get some frozen yogurt." And that woman would likely say, "Oh, cool!" Or perhaps, "NO, how about cheesecake instead."

With Hilda she'd instantly get upset. Then she'd break down the whole sentence in order to lecture me. (One thing I loved was, when she spoke, her accent would go up and down in a sing-songy way – like a karaoke ball bouncing through the words.) "Vhy did you TELL me to come vith you, and not ASK me to come vith you? And vhy did you pick JOGHURT and not ask vhat I VANTED for dessert?" It was a constant challenge.

On our first date, I wanted to take her somewhere nice. A place she'd never been. Something that really represents America. Naturally, I chose P.F. Chang's.

In Sweden, the women pay for their own meal, but I wasn't having it. When the bill arrived, I grabbed it Persian-style and paid in the blink of an eye. This made her very upset. "HEY! Vhy did you do dat?! That vas very rude."

In the car she revealed she didn't even like the food that much. I apologized and promised to take her somewhere nicer and even more American next time... "Olive Garden."

"Nicer?! NO! I don't vant these fancy places."

"Okay, no need to get upset. What kind of food do you want?"

"I vant to try the fast-food places. All the fast-food places in America."

Somebody please pinch me. Really?! Turns out this Swedish princess wasn't looking to be wined & dined like the typical LA girl. She wanted Jack in the Box, Arby's, Chik-Fil-A, and to experience this Burger King she'd heard so much about.

Well, in that case, why didn't ya just say so? I'M YOUR MAN!

We worked our way through date nights at the hottest spots our nation has to offer: El Pollo Loco, Carl's Jr, Subway and even Sonic Burger. She was all smiles. No more complaining. I'd cracked the code. Better yet, she demanded to pay half the time. It's like I'd hit the lottery.

Three months into our relationship, the reason we broke up was as foreign to me as she was. One afternoon I got a distressed call from her (just like every other day). She was on the verge of tears and once again it was my job to calm her down.

"Ok. Just, relax Hilda. What happened?"

"Vell, today I got to vork, den my friend called to tell me she vas sick. And I said, 'Oh, no! I vill bring you soup. So, I left vork to get soup for my friend. And den my boss is calling. He say, 'Vhere are you?' And I told him my friend vas sick, so I am bringing her soup. He told me, 'No, you are expected to be here at work. Get back here now or you are FIRED!' Can you believe he treat me like this?"

I took a deep breath, then tried to rationalize with her, "Hilda, in America we actually are not allowed to leave work. If your friend is sick you can send her soup or bring it to her *after* work."

She shrieked, "So, now you are taking *HIS* side!"

And with that she hung up. I never heard from her again. Sometimes when I'm at a Kentucky Fried Chicken I still think about her.

I sure am going to miss taking a perfect 10 to Taco Bell.

SCANDINAVIAN LOGIC

While dealing with a comedy club in Norway I came to the conclusion that Scandinavians are very fair people. Maybe a little *too concerned* with fairness. Here's why...

I was on the phone with a club owner in Oslo, planning what was to be my very first show there. I told her we should make the presale tickets $20. Then raise the price to $30 on the day of the show. This would entice people to buy early.

Our Norwegian friend was not having it.

"Nah. Dis goes against our business practice. Ve don't do dis to da customers. Dis vill make dem very unhappy."

Again, I explained the need to give people a financial incentive to pre-buy their tickets and ensure a guaranteed audience.

"$20 presale and $30 at the door is how I always do it all over the world."

She balked again in her Norwegian accent,

"Vell, I don't feel comvtorble with dis. So ve vill not. Ve vant everyone to be happy."

And with that, the call was over.

Norway is known as one of the happiest places on earth, yet I was going to bed upset. Here I am, 13 years into my career, I know what works and what doesn't. I was paying to rent their venue, and I was spending thousands in advertising and flights to get there. I should have a say over how I market my own show!

As I nodded off, I had a very stupid idea. I thought, no way will this work, *and* it was really going to irritate the Norwegian. Might even lose the chance to do a show there. But when I woke up, I decided, to heck with it. Let's give it a try. I called her back...

"Hi, I know we don't want to raise the price for the tickets."

"Yes, I told you dis yesterday."

"Right, well I had an even better idea. I was thinking – what if we make the tickets $30. But we LOWER the price $10 for anyone who buys them ahead of time. This way we give them a nice reward... Like a thank you."

I waited to get yelled at again by Miss Happiness. She considered it for a moment then squealed, "Yea, dats a very nice thing ve can do. And then they vill be so happy!"

"Absolutely. Everyone will just be – full of happiness."

"Okay, I vill do this pricing and ve advertise it on the vebsite!"

My god, it worked! I was now getting the exact same thing I'd asked for the day before. $20 presale. $30 at the door. Why was that so hard in the first place?!

Lesson learned. You can't always get what you want, but if you try sometimes – you might find – you get what you need... from Norwegians.

SAY YOU'RE CANADIAN

Immediately following September 11th in 2001, flights to Europe were $199 round trip. That's cheaper than driving! My family advised against going, but with prices so low, it was worth any risks that might come along with it.

The summer arrived, my bags were packed, and I took off with some pals on my Europa Touropa.

A recommendation I kept getting from college friends was to put a Canadian flag on my luggage. They said this would elicit nicer treatment from Europeans.

To that I said a common American phrase, "NO WAY, JOSE!"

Sure enough, when I arrived, I noticed a lot of "Canadians" milling around. I didn't exactly advertise I was American but didn't feel the need to go undercover either. As we crisscrossed Italy, France, England, and Spain, I realized that my group of buddies were approximately 5 inches taller and at least 30lbs heavier than most of the people we saw. If they wanted to disrespect us over our nationality, we'd just have to offer them a patriotic boot to their backside.

I was relieved to find this was the furthest thing from anyone's mind. We were treated great by everyone – *and in France, just as rude as everyone else!* I ended up in Spain on the 4th of July. A pub Ernest Hemingway used to frequent recreated an American flag out of shot glasses filled with mysterious Red, White & Blue liquors. They were free of charge and we drank and celebrated America's independence with a group of Spaniards.

The hospitality was great towards Americans who'd just been through tragedy and by the end of my trip, I was glad I hadn't taken the cowardly advice and sold out my country by pretending to be a syrup drinking neighbor-from-the-north.

To my foreign friends, please keep in mind: approximately 75% of the "really nice Canadians" you keep meeting are actually from the USA. College leftists should grow a pair and come out of the closet. Be like Benjamin Franklin, instead of shy away from who you are, become an exemplary citizen and change the minds of the people you meet. Let your behavior and warm smile do the talking. After all that, if someone still treats you rude you can always:

1. *Walk Away*

2. *Demonstrate what USDA grade muscle is all about*

3. *Simply accept the fact that you are most likely in France!*

GASOLIO

In Italy my friend and I decided to rent Vespas for the day. It was a blast and I highly recommend it as the best way to zip around Rome.

The time flew by. We needed to fill up our mopeds and return them or we'd face a steep late charge. Only one problem, it was Sunday as well as some sort of religious holiday to boot. This meant all gas stations were closed.

By the way, there are a lot of religious holidays in Italy. Every day they surprise you with a new one. Some holidays are observed only for a few hours. Someone of authority will walk up to you and say,

"We're closing."

"What? We just got here…"

"It'sa too bad-uh. We have to shut down in remembrance of San Domingo."

"What did he do?"

"He uh… This wasa the firsta… He helped the— You aska too many questions. It doesn't matter. Tha museum, isa closed. You can come-a back at noon."

Anyway, back to the mopeds. They were low on fuel and due back in an hour. I spotted a self-serve gas station, and although nobody was working that day, the pump still allowed me to swipe my card… *Win!*

I grabbed the nozzle and laughed that the Italian word for gasoline is GASOLIO. That's what it said right there on the pump. Seriously. If you want to speak Italian just add – *olio*, to any word.

I filled my mopedolio but it wasn't easy. The Vespa had this little hole to fill up the tank and the gas station had these big nozzles that wouldn't quite fit. It was annoying. I had to kind of hold it steady and shoot the gasolio into the tank. What a stupid country!

In a Mario Brothers accent I called out to my friend, "Mama mia, it's so harda to put Gasolioooo in the moped. Comma on. It'sa your turn."

He laughed and joined in, "Okay, Imma ready. Gimme the gaso-lio!" We skillfully shot the gas into his tank and we were ready to go.

That's when we realized we had a problem. I went to fire up my moped and it kept dying. My friend's Vespa started but was shooting horrible smoke out of the back. I tried mine again and nothing. We were panicked. How could our bikes both not be working at the same time?

Then it clicked. We both realized what had happened; *GASOLIO IS DIESEL!* It turns out *BENZINA* is the word for gasoline. That explains why the nozzle didn't fit. That's why his moped was polluting the air. And that's why my bike was now disabled. Had San Domingo not died or did whatever he had done on that day, we would have had some assistance at the pump, BUT NOOOOO...

I cursed San Domingo!

Now we had to get the diesel fuel OUT of the bikes. With all our strength we flipped each moped upside down and held them by the tires to try and drain it into the flower bed next to the gas station. We got some very nasty looks from the locals while doing this. One yelled at us,

"Stupid American assholio, why you pour the gasolio into the plantolios?! That's abad for the environment!"

We just smiled and waved,

"It's okay. WE'RE CANADIAN!"

Finally, we unhooked the benzina pump and filled up the bikes properly. Once again, my friend's moped started up right away but was still shooting out black smoke. Mine was useless. Soaked with the wrong fuel, it was going to be a lonnnng walk for me. It felt even longer as I pondered how much this ordeal was going to cost.

We arrived over an hour late for the return. That was an automatic $100 fee. Then they found out about the gasolio and claimed they would need another $500 per bike. Staring at a $1200 bill I came up with a theory. Italians are very passionate. If only we could be more passionate and upset than they were, perhaps we could meet somewhere in the middle.

The shouting went back and forth for 10 minutes. They spoke with their hands and so did I.

"I give you $600 for both bikes. Not a penny more! This was your fault AND the fault of San Domingo!"

They gasped, "Mama mia, not San Domingo!"

My friend and I threw the cash at the attendants and started slowly walking off, waiting for them to grab us by the collar and continue the debate, but it never happened. Perhaps they were tired from waiting all that time. Or perhaps they needed to get back to their family for the big holiday.

Either way, they seemed content with the cash, and I was happy we got out of there for half price and a great story to go with it.

Also, not entirely sure, but I may never be allowed back in Rome.

LAST-MINUTE HAWAII MARATHON

I arrived in Hawaii for Christmas break a day before the rest of the family. Checking in at the hotel, the receptionist asked if I was there for the marathon the next morning. I replied, "Nope, but my family doesn't arrive until noon. Maybe I'll jump in and do it."

She laughed at the idea, "Oh no, it's sold-out and you have to train for something like that."

I did a quick calculation. The marathon was to start at 5am and if I could finish in under five hours, I'd easily be able to meet the family at the airport by noon. With that, my mind was made up. No training, no entrance fee. Just join the sea of people and go for it.

By 4:30am I headed 2 miles to the starting point. There were approximately 35,000 people there and nobody was checking for my bib number. We were welcomed in Korean, Japanese, and English.

"ON YOUR MARKS, GET SET, GO!"

And with that, I embarked on one of the most amazing experiences of my life. The first hour, we ran in the dark. The cool ocean mist spraying into the air. Then we were met by a brilliant sunrise. 2 hours later the heat was intense. Locals lined the streets and offered water, juice, pineapple and even homemade Hawaiian baked goods.

I started out strong for the first 16 miles. The Kenyans were way out in front and a few athletic people moved further ahead, but I was holding my own. By mile 17 I was thinking, "Maybe I should have trained for this."

My shins, thighs, and hips were sore. On top of that, nobody warns you that your hands tingle and fall asleep from being in an upright angle for so long. I went from running to shuffling along.

Then things started getting embarrassing. The people that started passing me were diverse: Both skinny & fat. Young & old. Even a wide range of disabilities. I was truly humbled. I never stopped running but you couldn't tell by my speed. Just then, a 90 year old Japanese lady in flip flops grunted, "Outta my way!" as she shoved me aside. So mean!

On the final length I cheered up. Although I'd been passed by a few thousand people, I was still in the top 10%. At 4 hours and 10 minutes I crossed that finish line. Not bad for a first timer. I didn't place first and I definitely wasn't last.

That year, the couple who took last place did so on purpose and in style. They were a pair of professional ballroom dancers who did the tango together, nose-to-nose for the full 26.2 miles. It took almost 12 full hours of sweaty formal dancing... and while I was impressed with the man, it was the woman who did it backwards and in heels. RESPECT.

Dec 14th, 2014

Brett and Jenny Griswold
Danced the Honolulu Marathon
and Finished in 11:43:08

I headed yet another mile back to the hotel, showered, and met up with arriving family members. They were perplexed as to why I was walking like Frankenstein. I told them about the impromptu marathon and I'm not sure they believed me. It didn't matter anyway, they informed me the whole family would be doing a zipline tour. It was prepaid and I was expected to be there. This course was complete with four more miles of hiking.

In hindsight, it was probably a good idea that I kept my muscles and joints moving instead of laying on the sand like a beached whale for a week. The only salvation I got that day were those stations where I was able to fasten my limp body to the cable and fly over the landscape.

*TRAVEL HACK: LIGHTEN YOUR LAUNDRY LOAD

Laundry while traveling is such a hassle. Instead, pack quick-dry socks, Lycra underwear, and spandex shirts. These can be washed and dried easily in a sink.

CHAPTER 6: BLACK TRUMP SUPPORTERS

One year I received a call unlike any other. The man on the other end of the line asked if I'd be willing to perform standup comedy for a group of African-American Donald Trump voters.

My first thought, "This must be a prank." I was assured they were indeed a real group and was encouraged to check out their website. There they were. A faction I had no idea existed.

I told the gentleman I'd LOVE to be there. Now it was his turn to be shocked. He told me 27 other comedians in Los Angeles had refused and I was their last option. (That felt wonderful to hear. It's always good to be someone's 28th choice.)

You'd think Hollywood, which pays lip service to "diversity is our strength," would be happy to embrace this unique crowd of minorities. It turns out they're a lot more close-minded than they advertise.

Not me! I started preparing my act.

Here's a little secret about comedy – if your whole audience is on the same page, it's much easier to write jokes they'll like. It doesn't matter what *page* that is.

The flyer for the evening went out on social media and some fairly big-name comedians started a hate campaign against the event. They locked in on me, someone they have never met, and hurled insults. I guess they thought by "shaming me" I might buckle to their pressure and drop out like the other comedians. But here's how I operate – I'll perform for any group, any time. I'll do a comedy show for loggers on Sunday and tree-huggers on Monday, Jews on Tuesday and Muslims on Wednesday. Your personal quarrel is not MY business. Nobody criticized the caterer for serving food to these various groups. They didn't start boycotts against the hotel for allowing the meeting in their ballroom. Yet, they think entertainers are punching bags; fair game to try and destroy our lives or "cancel" us. That doesn't fly with me. At the end of the day we're all humans and probably share more similarities than differences. I gave all those haters the virtual middle finger and went back at them on social media with 3 rebuttals for every one they sent my way.

Since I didn't back down, they eventually gave up. The night of the show came and I took the stage, swinging for the fences to a sold-out crowd,

"Black Republican Trump Supporters? I didn't even know you guys existed. I see you all looking around... Looks like YOU didn't know you existed, either!"

They laughed.

"There's got to be some sort of law in LA County that you can't ALL be in the same building at the same time. You know the rules; one black Trump supporter per zip code. Let's go, spread out. Break it up before the Democrat Fire Marshalls get here."

They laughed harder. I continued,

"Some people wanted to be here but couldn't make it tonight. Elizabeth Warren wanted to be here, but she's too busy playing *Cowboys & Indians*. Bernie Sanders wanted to be here but couldn't find a balloon to comb his hair. Joe Biden would have been here but didn't want to fall up those stairs. Hillary Clinton was invited several times, but as you know, she lost all the emails."

EVERY JOKE DESTROYED.

After that I could do no wrong. They even said I was now an honorary Black Republican. I've never felt more accomplished.

NO MORE PARKING TICKETS

Living in Los Angeles, you might as well add "Citations" to your monthly budget. They're unavoidable and there are a thousand ways to slip up: Street sweeping, adjustable parking hours, flexible loading zones, scheduled construction, and more. Reading an LA sign is harder than taking the LSAT.

In Nevada, we always had plenty of free parking, so moving to California was quite the adjustment.

Photo tickets are even worse. For one, there are no left-turn arrows to help you cross at LA intersections. At least 5 times a year you'll find yourself stuck in the middle of a busy avenue attempting to frogger your way across the street. When the light turns red, instead of a grace period, there's a *FLASH*. Which lets you know your photo was just taken. That Polaroid will cost you $240+ once it arrives in the mail.

One time a friend asked for help going over an audition. I parked at her place for no more than 45 minutes. I returned to find a $750 ticket waiting for me. This wasn't a fire zone, there were no handicap postings. This should have just been a regular parking ticket at most! WHAT COULD IT BE?! Little did I know they have this thing called *anti-gridlock zones* between 3 and 6pm where the penalty is 10 times the standard rate.

Another time I read the signs very carefully and was sure I could park there. The next morning, I came out and my car was gone. Now, in LA that could mean any number of things, but this time the city was in on it. On the other side of a tree, they'd taped a "No Parking Tomorrow Only" sign. It wasn't visible from a driver's point of view. But did that matter to the city of West Hollywood? NOPE! They'd towed me and since they yanked my car on a Tuesday night and I picked it up Wednesday morning, that was 2 days at the impound for an extra $800. They pointed out I was still on the hook for the original $75 parking ticket once I got home.

That was the last straw. I was not going to let them ambush me with citations like that ever again. Instead, I devised a plan to avoid it entirely.

First, I took the license plates off my car and replaced them with the cardboard dealership inserts. If ever pulled over, I had the up-to-date plates in the trunk. "Officer, what a coincidence, my plates just arrived, and I was on my way home to screw these babies in." In reality, these would remain in the trunk permanently.

And with no plates on the car, no meter maid could ever write me a ticket again. But K-von, they can just go off your VIN number! Normally you'd be correct, but I may or may not have changed that, too. By changing the last digit of a vin, all tickets are written out to a car that doesn't exist.

Yes, it's a little risky. Okay, technically it's a federal offense, but repeat after me, "Officer, it was like that when I bought the car. I knew nothing about it and I will get that fixed as soon as I get home!"

*PARKING HACK — TAILGATER

Park in any major city for free. Big parking structures try to reduce expenses by utilizing an automatic payment system at the exit. By getting rid of a human attendant they save a lot of money... *USUALLY.*

Now, say someone in front of you is leaving and you simply tailgate them. The sensor might mistake you for a stretch limousine or something. That automatic arm won't come back down until you're all the way through. The longest I've made this little trick work was after a comedy show. I waved 14 cars through, bumper-to-bumper, for a combined savings of about $400 that night.

CRUISING FOR A BRUISING

Some people mock cruise ship comedians. "They're so cheesy!" What if I told you that's not necessarily the comedian's fault? I mean, most likely it is, but let me offer the following defense.

Cruise ships require the following schedule of their jokesters:

20 min Welcome Aboard performance = clean

45 min Family Show = clean

45 min Theater Show = PG13 to light R

20 min Farewell Performance = clean

We're told to refrain from bad language as well as making jokes about race, religion, politics, or sexuality. Also, try not to glorify drinking/drugs, no criticizing the cruise line, be careful when picking on the customers and staff, but other than that, *say whatever you want.*

Oh, great! Typically, the only comedians that can meet these restrictions are in their sixties and primarily work church gigs.

One particular night, a showcase was set up in Hollywood and all the major cruise lines were in attendance. I performed a ten-minute set and was promptly informed I'd secured 15 weeks at sea. Excited for a moment, I then cringed thinking of all the strict guidelines I'd have to adhere to. I didn't have that much material!

They were throwing me to the sharks without a life raft. It was going to be sink or swim. If I didn't get this right, it would be a titanic failure.

*Boom, 3 cruise references in a row!

Rehearsing all of the appropriate material I had with a stopwatch revealed I was coming up about 30 minutes short with no time to fix the problem. That first cruise I taaaaalked a lottttt sloowwwerr than normal in order to make it work. (The older audience members probably liked that better.)

At the same time, I walked around the ship with a notepad like a detective, jotting down ideas and trying to find humor in whatever I could. Making fun of the carpet, the destinations, the buffet line... anything to improve my cruise show and get back to speaking at a regular speed.

Around week four, I felt comfortable with the new schedule and found myself tightening up the set. I am now 30 cruises in and happy I took on the challenge. Plus, I can now work well past my 60th birthday.

Cruises feel like luxurious floating prisons to me. You get a small room. Your cell phone often doesn't work (which sounds horrible at first but becomes a bit of a luxury). Honestly, my productivity goes through the roof. Writing, organizing, editing videos, catching up on books, and organizing my thoughts: it's now become a welcome part of my comedy schedule. Not to mention it's an all-expense paid vacation.

CHAPTER 7:
MY COMEDY WILL
GO ON...

After 10 successful weeks at sea I'd really gotten the hang of it. I was ready to add a new level of difficulty. Spice things up a bit. What better way than by bringing a woman on board!

I was dating a doctor at the time and she loved her fancy cars, bags, and heels. The idea of a cruise was enticing for her. She worked long hours and deserved it. She hated that I was gone for extended periods of time and jealous of the destinations I would visit. For her birthday, I gave her a surprise. She would be coming with me aboard the Independence of the Sea.

I explained we would be visiting Aruba, Jamaica and I told her, "Girl I want to take ya to Bermuda, Bahamas. Come on pretty momma."
*She had no idea these were also the lyrics to a Beach Boys song.

Oh, and a little secret between you and I, as the headlining comedian she would be coming for *FREE!* Outside of the flight, this wasn't going to cost a dime.

The comedians typically get a regular cabin with a window. My girl asked if we should upgrade to another room with a balcony, but that wasn't offered on the free plan, so I quickly dismissed it. The room with the window would be more than adequate and we could use those extra funds on beach excursions.

One thing I didn't know, if the ship is sold-out they stick all comedians on Deck 1, the very bottom of the boat. Below sea level. This had never happened to me, but wouldn't you know it, of all the weeks I had been at sea this was the one and only time it reached full capacity. There would be no balcony. If there was a window, it would only be suitable for watching the fish swim by.

Embarrassed, I escorted my lovely date down 7 flights of stairs, past the boiler room, and into our tiny crew cabin. I'd never been this far down. We found a pair of narrow bunk beds awaiting that pulled down from a hinge on the wall. (I wanted her on top of me, but this wasn't what I had in mind.)

To make matters worse we were instructed to carry two badges at all times and wear a pin that said CREW MEMBER so that security would not harass us for being on Deck 1. She didn't want to do that and was lectured by staff each time they saw her breaking the rules.

Every morning we woke up at 5am to the sound of a dropping anchor which took place on the other side of our wall. Heavy chains cha-chug-cha-chuging for about ten minutes. Even worse, the smell of diesel exhaust filled up our room each time the engines fired up.

Sharing a tight cabin is hard enough on a new couple, and this was even worse. I tried to cheer her up and make the best of it. As we choked on the fumes, I told her we now had a funny memory we could look back on forever. Turns out I was right, because that was our last trip. She's long gone and all I have left is that memory!

PUSHUP BRA

I blame Dr. Phil for another relationship that ended abruptly. One day I was minding my own business when the bald mustachioed expert appeared on TV. In his thick southern accent, he said, "The couple that works out together stayyyyys together. It builds a bond. After all, yer' working towards a common goal."

That sounded good to me. I told my girlfriend at the time to get ready – we were heading to the gym! Everything was going great up until we got there. When it was time to run a mile to warm-up she said, "I *hate* cardio." We went to do lunges and she said "My knees hurt." I proposed pull-ups and I'd even support her legs. She said "Ew, no way." We were not building any bonds. One by one she shot me down. I suggested we do 10 pushups and just go home.

She protested, "I'm definitely NOT doing that."

"You won't even do 10 pushups? Why?!"

"Because, I don't want to get huge chest muscles. I think that looks manly and gross."

"You don't get huge muscles from 10 pushups. Bodybuilders work for years to achieve that. You think you'll turn into Schwarzenegger within one set?"

That was enough for her. She was ready to leave. Silence on the drive home. We had achieved no common goals. We had built no bonds. Once we got back to the house, I did an online search to prove my point: *Should Women Do Pushups?*

The results were all in my favor. One link revealed, women who do pushups regularly can build an inch of muscle underneath their natural anatomy. In scientific terms, that additional padding will make those hooters stick out a full inch further than before.

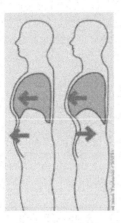

I ran over to share this new discovery with her. She was not amused. I've retold this story several times and women always take her side. They say I was rude, acted like a jerk, and one even said that it came off as very sexist.

Ladies, if there was an exercise that men could do to give us one extra inch of padding underneath our natural anatomy... we'd be on that machine daily, just for you!

The *DikBlaster 3000*. Why don't you go work on THAT, Dr. Phil?!

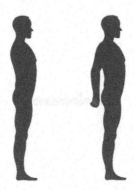

DESIGNER MUSCLES

While making a protein shake, I noticed the packaging proudly declared, "THIS PRODUCT WILL GIVE YOU THE DESIGNER MUSCLES YOU DESIRE." I thought about that for a moment. Designer muscles? I wanted real muscles. Functional muscles. I didn't *just* want them to look good.

I then considered my daily workout routine: Curls, pullups, pushups, and those battle ropes that you grab and yank up and down... Sadly, none of these would benefit me in combat. I may be able to bend down, grab my attacker's shoelaces, and pull on those for 45 seconds, but, but that'd be about it. (If he's wearing sandals or Crocs it will render me defenseless.)

CHAPTER 8: ORANGE BACKPACK

I'm in Santa Ana jogging on a treadmill, when I suddenly find myself laughing uncontrollably. What caused this outburst? The most mundane thing ever. It's hard to even explain.

To my left, a Hispanic man was getting off his treadmill. He threw his backpack on to go home. It was slightly unzipped, and three oranges flew out. That was it. Nothing really that funny about it, just oranges spilling out and rolling on the floor, but my comedian mind started to wander. Here I am, in a heavily Latino part of California and now I'm confronted with a bag full of oranges. I relayed this to a buddy later that day and he didn't think it was funny. I protested, "Come on, that's hilarious. Oranges?! In Orange County? Mexican guy... that's funny, bro!"

He disagreed, "Not only is it not funny. It's RACIST."

That's where I draw the line. Not every joke that involves a race or culture is RACIST. That word is used far too loosely these days. Let's take a look at the dictionary definition:

Dictionary

rac·ist

/ˈrāsəst/

noun

a person who shows or feels discrimination or prejudice against people of other races, or who believes that a particular race is superior to another.
"the comments have led to her being called a racist"

I showed no discrimination and in no way felt I was superior to the man with the rogue oranges. If you still think it's racist, I'll present another argument in my defense. Allow me to offer some other scenarios:

How funny would it be if a Hawaiian guy was next to you, threw on his backpack and 3 PINEAPPLES flew out.

It has nothing to do with skin color. Tell me you wouldn't laugh if an Irish guy were to throw on his backpack and 3 potatoes came tumbling out. And that's why I was giggling. I kept thinking of different scenarios. The possibilities were endless.

Imagine an Italian guy throws on his backpack, and out comes spaghetti, a meatball... and a handgun. Then he looks at you and says, "Shhh... Fughetabout it. Capice?" Brilliant!

Or a Japanese guy throws on his backpack and what falls out... Did you guess rice? Chopsticks? WRONG. The correct answer is homework and a calculator. Who's the racist now?!

The best part, you can come up with your own, like *Mad Libs.*
(Fill this out, share it on social media, and TAG me!)

a Polish person threw on their backpack and __a perogi__ fell out.

an Australian threw on their backpack and _____ fell out.

a French person threw on their backpack and _____ fell out.

a Canadian threw on their backpack and _____ fell out.

a Persian threw on their backpack and _____ fell out.

an Arab threw on their backpack and ____**RUN**____ .
We'll figure out what fell out later!

a Filipino threw on their backpack and _____ fell out.

a German guy threw on their backpack and _____ fell out.

a _____ threw on their backpack and _____ fell out.

I used to skip the black backpack when performing this joke
live, but one night a black guy called me out.

"You didn't do the black backpack!"

"Oh, sir I don't do that one because it may come off as racist."

"You did everyone else. If you don't do my backpack, THAT'S racist!"

We all laughed, and the crowd cheered me on. He was right,
if we're all equal then we all have a backpack. So, let's talk
about it.

"Fine. But you have to help me with the answer. What would come out of a black dude's backpack?"

To my surprise he yelled, "YOUR WALLET!"

It's safe to say he got the biggest laugh of the night.

Another way you know it isn't racist, most of these are simply *countries*, not races. The funniest one I ever came up with – RUSSIAN. We all know what would come out of a Russian's backpack... Not vodka. A *smaller* Russian with a smaller backpack. Then a smaller Russian with an even smaller backpack would fall out. Then an even smaller one... all the way down to a little baby Russian with a little tiny backpack.

In conclusion, it's not racist it's HILARIOUS. Your honor, I rest my case!

A VERY LATINO 2050

One reason I'd never criticize any one culture is because you never know who'll be in power next. It's always good to be on the right side of history. All forecasts predict Latinos will be the largest population in the USA by 2050.

I'm a forward-thinking guy, so I started working on my Hispanic-friendly jokes immediately. My goal is to be one of the top 3 Latino Comedians in the world by mid-century. I envision the list as follows.

TOP 3 LATINO COMEDIANS:

1. George Lopez
2. Gabriel Iglesias
3. K-von (by then I'll be known as 'K-abron.' Just a little nickname my Latino friends call me.)

As far as the jokes are concerned, I only have 3 so far, which doesn't sound too promising. Then again, 2050 isn't exactly right around the corner. Here they are mi amigos...

K-ABRON'S TOP 3 LATINO JOKES:

Q. Why do Latina's call you "Papi" in bed?
A: You're about to be a FATHER...

Q: What do you call it when you kiss a Latina's boobies too hard?
A: Dos-Hickies!

Q: What do you call a gay Mexican guy who keeps trying to hook up with your Uncle?
A: Tap-A-Tio.

All hits. Just need to write about 600 more and I'll be ready for 2050. Will you?

LET US PRAY

A group of eight Somalian ladies walked into the comedy club where I was about to perform. They wore the full covered garb. The whole outfit — *Bed, Bath, and Beyond!* They were polite, sat front & center, and were great sports as each comedian hit the stage and had fun with them.

In a way they became the stars of the show. It was now my turn. Everything seemed to be going just fine, but at one point they became distracted. I kept going but I did not have their undivided attention and as they were whispering to each other it was nagging at me.

Was my fly down? Had I offended them with a joke? Why were they nudging each other and breaking out into full blown conversation? My mind was racing. Then at the exact same time, all of them pulled their chairs out, stood up, and they spread out to various parts of the comedy club.

Rugs were unrolled and now I'm performing to a big hole of empty seats in the middle of the room as they proceeded to pray. After the show, I found out that they had to pray at that exact time every night.

Performing while people are praying made me incredibly nervous. And it's not because I thought a terrorist attack was coming or anything like that. I thought I was BOMBING. From a comedian's point of view, I'm wondering, "Am I doing so poorly they are asking a deity for help?"

In my head I felt the scenario went like this...

"These are his jokes? He's so much better on YouTube. This is most uncomfortable. Let's see if we an help... 'Oh Allah, please give him more Ha-Ha'!"

LITTLE ROCK MOSQUE

Years later I was invited to Little Rock, Arkansas to perform for a group of Muslims. This was a fundraiser to build a mosque near downtown. The room was seated with women on one side, men on the other. Obviously, a room like this would need very specific material.

But my first joke, I just couldn't help myself. I exclaimed, "Look at all these beautiful women. I'm surprised Bill Clinton isn't here tonight!"

Nobody seemed to laugh as hard as I did at that one. My next joke didn't do much better. I said, "Since this is a fundraiser to construct a new mosque, you actually have a lot in common with a Trump rally. We need to BUILD THE WALLS... BUILD THE WALLS!"

MEN'S HAIRCUT

Imagine my surprise when I went to a hair salon one afternoon and asked for a haircut.

The receptionist said with a smirk, "Well, we do have chairs open – but sadly we don't do men's haircuts. You'll have to go somewhere else."

I was new to the area, didn't know where else to go, and pressed for time, "Are you sure you can't slip me in just this once, do a quick haircut, and I'll just pay cash?"

She impatient, "NO, sir. As I told you, WE DON'T SERVE MEN HERE."NOW, PLEASE LEAVE."

Isn't that odd? Here I am, a guy with hair, who just wants it cut slightly shorter. Yet they were REFUSING to serve me based on MY GENDER. Why? What does gender have to do with a haircut? I was going to remain clothed the whole time. I didn't want any trouble.

Correct me if I'm wrong. It is illegal for businesses to refuse customers based on skin color, religion, or sexuality. It's illegal to refuse to let a girl in Boy Scouts or let someone of the opposite gender use a restroom.

There was a Christian baker who didn't want to design a gay wedding cake. Well, that went all the way to the Supreme Court. But it is totally acceptable to tell *me* to take a hike? Are men the last ones that can be legally discriminated against?

You likely don't really care about this situation. You are not looking to write your congressman. You don't feel the urge to protest this location. And I don't blame you. Realizing I was on my own, I'm proud to say I stuck up for MYSELF. As she stood there with arms crossed, I headed for the exit. Then paused and turned around one last time, "Excuse me, would you cut a woman's hair if she drove a SUBARU?!"

She shot back, "Well of COURSE!"

"Well, THAT'S THE SAME HAIRCUT I WAS GOING FOR!"

...and with that I slammed the door behind me. All I wanted was to get my hair looking like Ellen DeGeneres. Was that too much to ask?

THAT'S RACIST!

The PC police try to tell you what costumes you're allowed to wear for Halloween, which holidays offend them, and now they try to tell comedians which accents are allowed on stage.

If you are a comedian of color, the radical left invites you to do any accent and tell any joke you want. If you happen to be white (or ½ Persian) they immediately want to censor you.

It's part of some imaginary rules they've made up, designed to be purposely confusing so that they can cancel you at any time for any reason.

Somehow, Australia has worked overtime to develop the most politically correct atmosphere in the world. It makes me wonder how a nation originating from rough and tough convicts became so overly sensitive.

While in Sydney, a local offered to show me around. We ended up in an Indian restaurant and she asked, "What do ye think of the food?" I replied in a fun Indian accent, "Tha curry here, is bery good!"

She damn near jumped over the table to cover my mouth with her hand, "What was thyat?"

"What!? I'm just saying I like it."

"Yea, but you did it in an accent. What if someone heard you?"

"There's no one around, but after you jumped across the table, they sure are looking now."

In a thick Australian accent she warns me, "Nyeva, nyeva do that ageen."

"If we were at an Italian restaurant, would it be racist to say, 'I lika tha pastaaa'?"

"No, but that's a white person."

"So?"

"So, it's racist to do the voice of a brown person. NOT a white person."

Oh, god. It's exhausting being around leftists. Suddenly, the curry didn't even taste that good anymore.

HOW TO DO AN INDIAN ACCENT:

First of all, it can't be racist if you LIKE the accent. It's a great pick-me-up to speak with an Indian accent. The way it flows. The way it ends in a SMILE. Indians are some of the happiest people I've ever met.

I think if you speak with an Indian accent at least 20 minutes a day you will be less stressed. If someone cuts you off on a busy road and you yell, "HEY, JERKKK!" that negative energy will stick with you all day. But if you say in a thick Indian accent, "It's okay... cut me off, I don't care. We will all get there eventually, my friend!" It just might add years to your life.

On Monday mornings, don't wake up like, "Ugh, have to go to work again?!" Instead, hop out of bed with an Indian accent,

"Today I GET to go to work! I can't wait to go to work. I might even work from 7 to 11!"

Much better.

Obviously, the Indian accent is peaceful. These are the people that invented yoga, for crying out loud! The question you may ask, "Yes, K-von I agree with you, but how do I do a good Indian accent?"

I came up with a simple device to help. Just pretend your mouth is on a roller coaster ride. Picture your favorite roller coaster and talk as if you are going up and around. This means you start lowwww... then GO UP REALLY FAST... do a loop-ty-loop... AND then come back DOWN again.

One of my comedian friends is Indian. He pulled me aside and said, "That doesn't sound very authentic."

"Oh, come on you have to be kidding?"

He said, "No, doesn't sound Indian at all."

"There are 1 billion of you. This has to be ONE OF THEM."

"I think you should leave."

I replied, "Nah-Imma-Stay."

PAPER STRAWS

Strolling the streets of San Francisco, I decided it was time for a beverage. I'm a huge fan of Boba, the milk tea that surprises you every few sips with balls in your mouth. (Ok, that didn't sound right, but that's exactly what it is.)

Tapioca balls sit at the bottom of the drink and the straw needs to be fairly large in order to suck them up. They are chewy, sweet, and delicious.

Little did I know, San Francisco had passed a new law banning the use of plastic straws. The reason; someone on social media found a turtle washed ashore with a straw stuck in its nose. The video of the straw-nosed-turtle quickly went viral as a cry against humanity. This was OUR FAULT. Things needed to change. And who was first with the knee-jerk reaction? The Bay Area of course. They dictated there would be no more plastic straws allowed and started their "Save The Turtles" campaign overnight.

That's all fine and dandy, however Boba is a drink that requires a lot of suckage to enjoy. A paper straw just doesn't have the same feel or power. In fact, paper straws, if we are being honest, SUCK. Or... don't suck. Look, I'm just as confused as you are here.

> Sip #1: This sip is fine. You think, "Wow this has a different texture... but we're saving the turtles!"

> Sip #2: The straw is a little soggy now. For women (or San Francisco men), it has now absorbed your lipstick color. Not good... but it's for the TURTLES!

> Sip #3: The straw is a little warped now. It's collapsing in on itself and no longer holding its form. Remember the turtles.

Sip #4: The straw is now limp. It could really use a Viagra right now... but you love the turtles.

Sip #5: This is no longer a straw. It's coming apart on your lips. You're no longer a fan of turtles.

Had this happened to hundreds of turtles, then I'd be on board, but ONE? Perhaps this was just a very dumb turtle. In fact, a straw is a snorkel. This should have helped him breathe. How come he couldn't make that work?

These were just a few of the thoughts I had as I sucked and sucked, trying as hard as I could to get balls in my mouth on the streets of San Francisco.

*TRAVEL HACK: TAKE HOME THE TOILETRIES

When you get to the hotel, tell them you forgot your toothbrush. Many provide a travel kit that would cost $3 at any gift shop. Next, grab the hotel shampoo, conditioner, lotions, even the dish soap if they offer it, and take those home, too. Now you can provide actual 'hotel accommodations' to your guests.

CHAPTER 9: NOW I KNOW MY GAY-B-C'S

A student in Pennsylvania is yelling at me. She's got a finger in my face and she's not backing down. This is what you can expect these days from your typical college activist.

I was performing at a university gig in Hershey, PA. At one point I asked, "Where's all my LGBTQ people at?!" They cheered, I did a few jokes for them, then moved on. I thought it had gone well but apparently I was wrong.

After my performance, this woman approached and started in on me right away.

"That was very rude of you to say, 'Where's all the LGBTQ people?' Seriously?!"

"Why? I didn't say anything bad about them?"

She stepped forward "Because it's LGBTQIAA+"

I was at a loss, "What's IAA+?"

She shrieked at my ignorance. Her friend pulled her back and they took off, shouting expletives over their shoulders and waving goodbye to me with one finger.

Rattled, I still didn't know what 'IAA+' meant, yet was determined to find out.

I will now share it with you, so you never accidentally find yourself on the wrong end of a lesbian's finger (unless you're into that).

We all know LGBTQ (lesbian, gay, bi-sexual, transsexual, and queer), but much like your iPhone they have recently done a few updates.

I = Intersexual
That just sounds like someone ready to get lucky in outer space. To boldly go where no man has gone before. Open to alien love on an intergalactic scale. Count me in!

A = Asexual
Someone who gets intimate with themselves. Sadly, during the whole pandemic that was me as well. *I'm killin' it with these new letters!*

A = Ally
This means you're a "friend" of all the other letters. NO FAIR. They're doing all the heavy lifting and you're just like, "I'm with them?!" I don't think so.

+ = Plus
Buckle up, the door is wide open for a lot more letters, symbols, and emojis. This isn't going to end anytime soon.

To appease people like my verbal attacker in Pennsylvania, I've created a catchy song to show how open minded I am. Sing it aloud to really get the feel of it...

♫ "LGBT S U V, WX – Y & Z...

Now I know my gay-bc's.

Next time won't you pee with me?" ♫

BANANAMAN

A lot of people have questions about my name. Who came up with it? Why is it K-von? Did you make that up? I will quickly explain it from beginning to end.

My real name is pronounced Kay-Von. But the parents decided to spell it Kevan. In reality it is spelled کیوان, but very few people can read that. Over the years, people had so much trouble pronouncing it – I wrote it phonetically to make life easier on all of us = K-von.

My dad is Iradj. He has a brother named Touraj. I suppose had they kept going they would have named their boys Threeraj, Fouraj, Fiveraj. If one was gay, perhaps "Garage" and they just don't let him in the house.

It's important to note that these names come from ancient Persia, and all Persian names have a meaning. Ask an Iranian what their name means and they'll be very excited to explain it.

"Hey Ghazaleh, what does that lovely name mean?"

She will pull you aside, dim the lights and tell you the tale.

"It is the most beautiful baby deer, able to run through the meadow with grace. Ghazaleh!"

"What about you Niloufar?"

"I am named after an elegant flower that against all odds was able to grow under the most harsh of conditions and flourish."

Sometimes I think they should update the meaning of these names to something more modern.

"Hey Amir – what does your name mean?"

"The guy who dropped out of community college, but was able to open his own auto-body shop despite his parent's protests and now has 3 successful locations in Northridge!"

I bet by now you're sitting on the edge of your seat wondering what K-von means. Behold; it is *The God Who Rules Over the Planet Saturn*. Pretty cool, huh?

This made me curious. If every name has a meaning, what did my last name, MOEZZI – translate to?

I searched and found nothing. But through extensive investigation I came to find that 'moez' in Farsi, means BANANA. If something is very Moez-Y, it's a very big and powerful banana. Therefore, roughly translated my name means:

THE GOD WHO RULES OVER SATURN W/ HIS GIANT BANANA

Now you know.

K-VON MO-EAZY

It's 5am. I'm in the Atlanta airport and surrounded by TSA agents who are dying laughing...

Having a unique name can be a blessing and a curse. Early on, I learned I could often make black people laugh simply by telling them my name. My success rate so far hovers around 100%.

I told my friend this fact and he refused to believe it. We were up at some awful hour in the morning, standing in line to go through the airport security and he challenged me, "Let's see if you can make that guy laugh."

The African American gentleman at the podium was checking ID's and didn't look like he wanted to be there.

It was my turn to approach. I handed him my ID and said, "Let's see if you can pronounce my name."

He raised an eyebrow, unamused, "Kevin?"

I gave it a little swag, "Nope... That's K-Vonnnnnn"

He kinda smiled, "For real? Ha. I like that. Kay-Vaughhnn. Okay!"

I'd already won. But that wasn't good enough. I said, "Try my last name..."

He focused, "Hmm, Moe... is that Mosey?"

"Come on dawg. That's MO-EAZY"

That's when he lost it, "Ha! Stop lyin'. Yo' name is Kay-vaughhnnn Mo-Eazy?"

"Yup!"

"For real? Mannnn, how did you get a black name?"

"That's a Persian name!"

"Not in Atlanta. If yo' name Kay-vaughhn Mo-Eazy out here, YOU BLACK!"

Now, I'm laughing. His coworkers are laughing. I acted out a cool little pimp limp as I headed to the scanner. This received an even bigger response. Then I put my arms up and prepared for the x-ray.

That's when he shouted, "According to this... you ain't black after all!"

Everybody laughed.

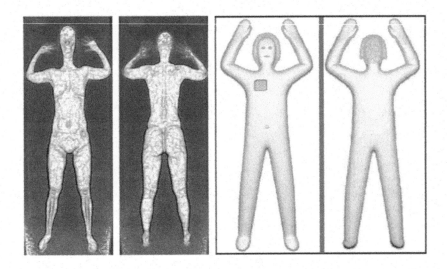

In my defense it was extremely cold standing on that tile with no shoes. I wasn't feeling very *Mo-Eazy* at that particular moment.

But, like I said, 100% success at getting the laugh.

SEXY PICS

Sexy pictures are a woman's domain. When they share them, people enjoy taking a peek. Women will even take the time to setup a photo shoot just to ensure the quality.

You'll never hear two men talking, "Hey Bob, watcha up to this weekend?"

"Just picking outfits for Sunday. Doing a boudoir shoot, you know, just to have it for when I'm older... you should swing by! My photographer is great."

Women's bodies look better. Any angle. Any outfit. Any occasion. Ladies, you keep sending and we'll keep gawking.

Men don't really know how to pose and it's not our fault. We don't have a lot of examples to go off of. Open a men's magazine and it's full of pictures of women. Now, open a women's magazine, and guess what... MORE WOMEN!

There are also ramifications for taking racy photos as a man. Look at Congressman Anthony Weiner, for example. He was simply trying to send exactly what his last name was suggesting to a special someone, but nooooo. It soon was made public.

That's right, someone leaked Anthony Weiner's wiener. After that he lost his job, his wife, his credibility, and his ability to succeed in public life.

Jeff Bezos, Brett Favre, Hunter Biden – the rogue photo shoots never end well. Even Jeffrey Tubin of CNN accidentally shot some unfortunate footage for the group during one of his boring online conference calls. He forgot the camera was on and was temporarily fired for spicing things up with his spicy little sausage.

That's why I encourage men to take a different kind of seductive photo. Why risk it with your biscuit?

What if I told you there are photos you can take that maintain your innocence yet still drive her wild?

"How?" you ask. By putting *more clothes on*. Women don't want to see you bending over on the beach, spread out on a sofa, or dolled up on your outdoor deck. Instead run to your closet and put your nicest clothes *ON*. Your best dress socks, slacks, button down, tie, shoes, belt, and coat. You heard me, guys.

Women don't want to see your booty; they want to see your booty headed to work. Unemployed guys just lounge around. Instead, snap a selfie on your way out the door with briefcase in hand.

*If you really want to drive her wild, make sure your 401k is dangling out.

*TRAVEL HACK: LIFEGUARD SHORTS

As an ex-lifeguard, I hung on to my trunks and bring them everywhere. Wearing them has come in handy. Unlike every other 1st responder, it's not illegal to impersonate a lifeguard. Those shorts present an image of authority. They've allowed me to skip the line at public beaches, waterparks, and Vegas pool parties. Simply make small talk with the gatekeeper, let them know you usually get in free, and 99% of the time they will thank you for your service and step aside as you enter the aquatic zone. Get a pair and make a splash.

CHORN

The "dressing up to take a sexy photo" joke has been so well received that I've decided to take it a step further. Let's make this book a little more ADULT, shall we?

Every gentleman reading this should create a calendar for their special gal. Follow me on this... 12 months. 12 nice outfits. Doing 12 different chores.

You already know what she likes, now it's time to execute:

~Doing the dishes in a flannel
~Vacuuming in a tux
~Cleaning the top of that fridge in a fireman's outfit...

The options are endless. This isn't just a handy desk calendar. It's what women want. It's Chorn!

LOST IN TRANSLATION

In Berlin, I sat in the back of a cab, and with the help of my driver, tried to pronounce the strange German words on the billboards:

"Wässer Män... Oh, like a water store or something? Water Man?"

"Yes, yes, my friend!"

"Deütsche Post... is that a German postage & shipping?"

"Yaaa."

"Uh huh, ßier Gärten... ok, that's like an outdoor pub!"

"Das correct."

"Oh what's this one, Dil... Dök-ing?"

The cab driver started laughing. What was so funny?

"My friend, das un adult store."

It suddenly made perfect sense. To my absolute horror, I'd been struggling aloud to sound out "DILDO KING".

GERMAN RECYCLING

Germans are huge on recycling. In Konstanz (a little town bordering Switzerland), I found myself in a beer garden. The beer was $5 but if you brought the bottle back, they'd give you $1.

(Compare that to the USA where bottles have a return deposit of 10 cents, and you're required to drive across town to collect it!)

Better yet, this exchange was all done right at the bar! I did the math and immediately went from casual drinker to businessman.

I started approaching tipsy patrons at tables littered with empty bottles. The drunks had long forgotten about the $1 deposit, but not I. After some small talk, I'd casually walk off with a bottle or two in each hand, return them, collect my cash, and go chat up a different group. I must have made about 30 trips.

After that was tapped out, I began twerking my way toward any empty bottles left behind on the dance floor. Oh, there's a bottle in the corner, time to do the Running Man and get over there quickly. Someone just left a bottle on the stage, I did the Roger Rabbit and swooped that one up, too.

Back to the return station I went, again and again.

It was the most fun I've ever had at a club. While others were dropping cash, I turned a night of drinking into a tidy profit. The opposite of *making it rain*. I collected the hail.

SELLING CANDY BARS

Finding new ways to make money has always been a hobby of mine. In elementary school, I remember taking my little red wagon around the neighborhood and removing soda cans from recycling bins. They were all lined up on the street weekly, I simply needed to pillage these items before the trucks came around. It was like shooting fish in a barrel.

Once I'd filled up a few garbage bags, my shift was over. I would roll the wagon home and Mom would drive me to the local recycle center where they'd weigh and pay around $17. That was big money for a kid.

A few months in, my business hit a bump in the road. A neighbor came out of the house and yelled, "Hey kid, stay out of my trash. If I see you again, I'm calling the police!" What a jerk. I told my parents about the situation and that was the end of that business venture.

In high school, class was significantly cutting into my ability to turn a profit. I was going to have to find a way to monetize the 7 hours a day consumed by school, but how?

It occurred to me – students love candy. I could buy items from Target for $.22 each and sell them for $.50. The candy machines on campus had a limited selection but the options I could provide were endless. Each day I'd fill a large Ziplock bag to the brim with all the best-sellers. By setting it on top of my backpack the items sold themselves. Twix, M&M's, Paydays, you name it. Inevitably someone would whisper, "Psst... what's up with those Rolos?"

Ready to make a deal, I'd whisper back, "2 for a buck."

Next, a dollar bill would slide my way under a shoe. Word started getting out and I was gaining popularity. Girls would wink at me... "Hey Candyman!" I had respect in the streets. I would throw a bully a Milky Way for some protection here and there. (Had to grease a few hands but it was a living.)

Heading to PE at 7am before school started was prime time. Those kids loved to start their day off wrong with Starbursts and some 3 Musketeers. It got to the point where I started packing several gallon-sized Ziplock bags to keep up with demand. Taking requests. Keeping track of inventory. I had my regulars and would offer free candy for those that made bulk purchases or gave referrals.

At the height of my operation I was clearing $60 a week in pure profit. Plus, I had two Freshmen under me selling in small batches. I was building an empire. That is, until I was called into the Vice Principal's office. I'd become too big. Word of my candy cartel had spread too far.

Like any dealer, it's important to know when to get out. And like many dealers, you don't know when that is until it's too late. There, in the office, I was faced with two angry cheerleaders who'd blown the whistle.

What did they care? Turns out a lot. Their team fundraiser involved selling KitKats and Reese's (and nobody wanted that crap at $2 a pop). I had been offering a better product at a better price and was going to be punished for it. I also learned that the reason schools don't sell Skittles or Starburst is these candies are easy to throw, causing even more disruptions in class.

That's how I got flagged in the first place. They discovered unauthorized projectile candies flowing through the school like water. I received a cease & desist from Vice Principal Coronado and that was the end of that. Foiled again. It was time to come up with a new way to make some cash.

HIGH SCHOOL BLUES

Senior year of high school is supposed to be a fun time; partying and bidding farewell to friends as you make plans for the next stage of life. I was a swimmer with a state tournament coming up. After that it was time to walk the stage and take my diploma.

With 2 months to go, my arch nemesis – Vice Principal Coronado – bulldozed her way into our classroom. She looked like Alice from the Brady Bunch. Short hair, khaki pants and was always on a mission to stop some fun somewhere. This day was no different. She stood in the front of the room and announced, "Folks, we have a report that someone in the Senior class is making fake ID's. If anyone knows who's doing this, please let me know."

This was the first I'd heard of it, and realized I needed one myself, so I blurted out, "But please let *ME* know FIRST!"

The whole class roared with laughter. As I look back, this may have been the beginning of my comedy career. The rush was amazing. What came next was not.

"You, OUTSIDE!"

Mrs. Coronado took me out of class, pushed my back up against the wall and threatened me with a finger in my face, "This is a serious thing buddy. It is a felony, a federal crime, and to think one of our Seniors would make a joke like that when you're supposed to be a leader on this campus?! One more outburst like that and you aren't graduating!"

The message was clear. The comedy career was going to be placed on hold. There would be no more attempts at humor that semester.

As I walked to my car at the end of the day, I noticed the windshield had been smashed and five local tough guys standing around. The leader was sitting on my hood.

I was not in the mood to be messed with and had a good buddy with me, so we sized up and decided to confront the whole group.

"What the &@$# are you doing on my car?"

"PJ just got arrested."

"Who the f@$# is PJ?!"

Things were tense. Turns out PJ was the guy making fake ID's. The Italian tough guy I'd never seen in my life did all the talking, "We was told yous went out in the hall and had a talk with Mrs. Coronado. Then 2 hours later PJ goes to jail... You ratted him out."

How do you like that?! Not only did a gag get me in trouble with the administration. I was now embroiled in a gang war with the worst kids in school. The kind who were headed to prison not Princeton.

I tried to defend myself in the parking lot court of justice, "I didn't tell on PJ. I said *I WANTED* an ID from PJ."

It didn't matter, the gang leader had already found me guilty. He put his hands up to start the boxing match and came toward me. I shoved him back and had my fists up. I looked around to find a circle had formed around me and noticed nobody was rooting for me on this one.

"Get em, Rocko!"

"Beat him up Rocky!"

My mind was racing. Minutes ago, I was casually walking to my car. Now, I have a smashed windshield and am somehow involved in a street fight.

We circled. Nobody seemed to want to throw the first punch. (Although, I was evading more than pressing the fight.)

Just then – here comes Mrs. Coronado, flanked by the school police. She entered the fray armed with her clipboard and whistle. Everyone scattered leaving me standing there alone.

This saved me from a potential beat-down but didn't do any favors for my street cred. The bullies were now certain I was colluding with Mrs. Coronado. Meanwhile, she could not understand why after her implicit warning to behave, I was now squaring off in her school parking lot.

The whole damn thing was Shakespearian. For the final eight weeks of my High School career, mysterious cars would follow me on the roads, people would threaten me at various places, and some graduation parties weren't attended due to the mixed company that might arrive.

...All because of a perfectly timed joke!

ROUND TWO, FIGHT!

The police are spread thin in Los Angeles. There are just too many people and far too much crime for law enforcement to do an effective job. Add to that a city quick to sue and jail their own law enforcement officers, and now the police would rather show up to fill out a report/count bodies instead of risk stopping a crime in action.

Ever seen a car chase on TV? We get about 2 of them per month in Los Angeles. Criminals evading police on the roads aren't much cause for alarm. Plus, it's great ratings for the media. They simply shut down the freeway, get the news helicopter in the air and make a day of it.

A criminal can take a final joy ride on a Friday from San Diego to Santa Barbara while plowing into cars, children, and mail-boxes along the way. The police are so ineffective, they'll even wait for a suspect to stop, fill-up, check the fluids, get an oil change, and then return to the "chase".

My father had purchased a classic Cadillac and let me take it to LA for the weekend. I was excited to cruise the Sunset Strip and potentially turn some heads. All was going well until I got to a red light on the crowded boulevard. Just then, an old Chevy truck slammed into me from behind.

Ugh... REALLY?! I got out to exchange insurance info with the driver, but the guy wasn't having it. He threw it in reverse, then peeled out around me.

ARE YOU SERIOUS!?!

I jumped back in the Caddie and pursued him. Even got into oncoming traffic for a moment then swerved back over so I was now behind the offender once again. I walked up to the driver's side, and it was clear he wasn't aware I'd caught back up. I banged on his window to his surprise.

"Out of the truck. Insurance or I'm calling the cops."

He mouthed some choice words that indicated he didn't plan to comply.

I had his license plate, but the fact that he dented the *Dadillac* and was brazen enough to leave the scene meant I would need to get some retribution.

I landed a solid kick to his door which changed his mind. Turns out he DID want to get out of his truck after all! That's when I realized I didn't really know how big this guy was. (He was seated after all.) Therefore, I needed to even the odds just-in-case.

As his one leg hit the ground, I took the opportunity to boot the door one more time, pinching his knee in process. That worked well, but he was still coming. When the next leg came out, I gave the door a final hard kick for good measure. I hoped that did the trick, because from that point on it would be 'Mano a Mano'.

At this point, we'd caused a scene that looked like something out of the video game Street Fighter: Two parked vehicles blocking heavy traffic on a Friday night, cars blaring their horns, vibrant billboards up and down the block, and onlookers with drinks in hand taking notice.

I was able to take inventory of my opponent for the first time. He was big, but visibly drunk. Now on two wobbly deer legs, he made his move. First, he took a big arching swing toward my head. Oddly enough, everything seemed to be happening in slow motion. I ducked under and watched his fist fly by. The other arm came toward my temple as I once again did the same half-squat maneuver I'd learned in my cardio-kickboxing class.

As I came back up, I threw my first and only wide-arching hook shot. It caught him in the temple and "Down went FRAZIER." That actually worked? I couldn't wait to tell my Zumba instructor!

The valet parking attendants from a bar nearby poured into the street to pull us apart. From their point of view, *I* had instigated the whole thing. I was trying to explain to the mob by yelling, "Drunk driver!"

They picked the defeated man up off the ground, dusted him off and put him back in his truck, encouraging him to get out of there. I protested, "NO! HIT & RUN!"

Alas, it was too late. I was left sulking in my dented car. I called 911 and explained what had just happened. The officer on the other end said, "Sir, how bad is the damage?"

"I don't know."

"Sir, we're really busy tonight so if you don't want to escalate this, you really don't need to."

I was shocked, "But there's a drunk driver on the road. So, like... do you want his license plate or...?"

He sighed, "Fine – what is it...?"

I rattled it off to the unenthusiastic cop and we ended the call. After that interaction I was glad I took matters into my own fists and got something out of it. I don't recommend becoming a street fighter, but that time it worked out. I'm currenty 1–0 on the Sunset Strip and hope to keep it that way.

*TRAVEL HACK: TIP THE STAFF

I always keep $2 bills on me. These rare notes are considered good luck and make for great conversation starters. Best of all, there's a misnomer that they're more valuable. In reality, you can visit any bank and exchange your cash for leftover $2 bills. Even if you were supposed to tip $10, impress valet with a $2 and drive off.

ONLINE DATING

Ideally you find the one person you love and live happily ever after. However, performing in a new city every few days can make that reality hard. With that said, it has never been easier to find single people on the road. It's as easy to get a date as it is to get an UBER. Just open up your phone and see who is in town.

Women will have the most luck in this department. For this reason, they are pickier. The average girl has a dating profile that says who she is looking for, what interests she hopes to find, an age-range, and the quality of character. They often list a minimum height requirement as well to ward off any applicants who are not tall enough to ride that ride.

Men's profiles are wide open. 18 to 99. Who are we to judge? Let's see what's out there. (Wondering why 99? Because it doesn't go any higher – I've tried!)

If you've never seen a dating app, it simply shows you a picture and you swipe their face left for "NO, get out of here!" or right for "YES, I'd like to meet that person." If you swipe NO they're gone forever. I like to picture the woman exploding wherever she is when I swipe LEFT. In a work meeting? Not anymore, BOOM! I wish we had that power in real life. If someone annoys you in a social setting, wouldn't it be great to just swipe LEFT on their face and watch them disappear?!

When women swipe it's, "NO... Hmmm, NO... Eh, maybe... Wait, NO."

When men swipe it's, "YES. YES. YES!" across the board. This can be done while driving or holding a conversation.

Matching with someone is only half the battle. Eventually you have to try and meet up. This is where other issues can arise. There have been horror stories of showing up and it is an entirely different person sitting there. That is called a CATFISH in the dating world. Nobody wants to be catfished. You have wasted time and energy on this person and now they have violated that trust.

Sadly, I've been on a number of online dates and I am here to tell you there are other things that can go wrong. For instance, it could be the same person, but they have gained a bunch of weight since they last took photos. I call this a BLOWFISH.

Or the girl could be wearing way too much makeup... CLOWNFISH.

You could be expecting to meet up with a white girl and turns out she's black... LITTLE MERMAID.

Worst of all, what if you show up to meet a beautiful girl and you realize it's actually a man.

That, my friends, is a SWORDFISH. You have been warned!

CHAPTER 10: MAGIC BULLET

Eating healthy on the road can be a huge challenge. But instead of making excuses, it's best to make adjustments. I bought a small blender and started packing it in my suitcase. Then once I land in a town, my first stop is to a local grocery store for some fresh produce. This cuts back on so many fast-food meals.

One time I was flying to 2 cities in 2 days. After day one, I headed to the airport realizing I'd bought too many items that were just going to go to waste. I threw the strawberries, spinach, carrots, and orange juice in my bag and checked it in.

Once we landed, I noticed a Dunkin Donuts by the baggage claim area calling my name. My friends all lined up to get one. As my bag dropped on the carousel, I decided to do the right thing. I walked over to the nearest electrical outlet, unzipped my bag, plugged in my blender, and whipped up a delicious smoothie. My friends were laughing that I'd just opened up my own personal Jamba Juice right next to the donut cart. For the rest of the tour I was called "Blender Boy."

Yes, I looked ridiculous, but I was able to skip a donut breakfast, winning a small victory against the battle of the bulge.

*Side Bonus: After skipping 3 overpriced airport meals, your blender has paid for itself.

MOTO CRASH

The traffic is so bad in LA that a twelve-mile drive might take up to two hours. It is for this reason I purchased a 2012 Harley Davidson motorcycle. Black.

Finally, I could get from point A to B in the proper amount of time. In California it is legal for motorcycles to cut between cars. This is because many motorcycles have air-cooled engines. They can overheat if they just sit there idling. It also entices more people to ride.

Even though it is totally legal, jealousy gets the best of many people stuck in traffic. They will scream, throw things, or even try to spit on bikers as they go by.

I even had one person tell me, "Oh yea, I hate bikers. I swerve my car into their path to teach them a lesson. Because if I didn't notice them, I might have hit them." I was flabbergasted. "So, because they're following a law you don't like, you risk *purposely* killing them so that you don't *accidentally* kill them." Ironically, if all the people on the road were on two wheels, then nobody would be stuck in traffic at all.

The motorcycle became my vehicle of choice for getting around California. The weather is great year-round, and you almost forget that it may actually rain sometimes. One night this happened while coming back from Orange County.

I'd never ridden under these conditions and decided to call my dad for some last-minute advice. "Hey Dad, what happens if it starts raining when I'm on the motorcycle?" His reply, "You get wet." Thanks Dad. He added, "Stay cautious, keep your speed down, and as long as there are no major flood zones, you'll be fine."

Doing just that, I was indeed soaked but made my way down the freeway. As my final exit approached, I started to change lanes. To my surprise, each time I crossed a painted white line my back tire would fishtail. Just my luck! To get this far and go down with only a few miles left. Luckily, I was able to regain control of the bike each time and get home safely.

One year later, I wouldn't be so lucky. I was scheduled to perform at a small wine bar. The show paid a measly $30 but would be a good chance to work on my new jokes. I hopped on the Harley and rumbled up the 101.

Having never been there before, I noticed my exit was coming sooner than expected. I cut across a few lanes to take it. Little did I know this was the only exit in all of Southern California with a 3 inch raised black curb, the exact same color as the freeway, dividing it.

The bike slammed into that curb which helped alert me it was there. That would have been nice to know beforehand. As I flew off the bike I thought, "Why didn't they paint it yellow?" After I bounced the first time I pondered, "Maybe putting reflectors on it would have been a good idea." By the third bounce I could see my bike heading down the road on a ghost ride, shooting sparks up into the air thinking, "That looks kind of pretty." Then I blacked out. Moments (or minutes) later, I was back on my feet talking to onlookers who'd kindly chosen not to run me over. I jogged to my bike and asked for a hand lifting it up. I also noticed a lot of broken car parts littered around. Apparently, I was not the only one who had not seen that asphalt curb. An ambulance arrived but I was in no mood to hop in their vehicle and add another $6,000 bill to this adventure. Body parts seemed to be working, so I mounted the bike and took off. The paramedics were not happy to see this, "SIR, Sir, wait... DON'T GO!" They must have been working off commission, but I was out of there.

I still had a show to do. I limped in 20 minutes late, looking like I'd slept in a garbage bin the night before. For the first time, I had enough light to evaluate the damage. My motorcycle jacket and helmet were shredded but had done their job. Even my shoe had a hole worn into it. By some miracle I'd put on double layer socks that night which were down to their final threads. The bike was dented and dinged up (but only on one side) and I had just installed a bar around the engine that ended up protecting it. Glad I added that! I was shivering partially from my extended time out in the cold and the rest from adrenaline/shock. The people who hired me asked what the heck happened...

"Uh, I was just involved in a motorcycle crash."

"What the... do you want to go home or need to go to
the hospital?"

"Actually, my $30 and a glass of wine sounds amazing right
about now."

A couple hours later, I'd completed my performance as planned
and asked the comedians to follow me home in their car to make
sure I made it back safely. The next morning, the pain got worse. I
was positive I'd broken ribs, or ankles, but the x-ray revealed the
only broken bone in my body was my pinky. Who falls off a Harley
and breaks a PINKY?! That's the least manly injury possible. The
bones were so small that the remedy called for hammering pins
into my finger and letting it heal for a few months. FUN!

Did that stop me from riding? Nope! I just don't go near that
exit anymore.

Heaven forbid anything happens to a single/unmarried person
under 30. If married, your significant other can clear out your
belongings. But if you're single, most likely your mom & dad will
have to handle that task.

Those who are single all have at least one thing in their room they
wouldn't want their parents to find. Some of you are now realizing
you have a whole bag or two full of unsavory items and objects.
That's why they need a new app where, if your heart stops, it
alerts a geek squad who can gain access to your place and dispose
of the previously agreed upon items quickly, before the family
arrives. This would save a lot of embarrassment, even though you
wouldn't be around for it anyway.

BUMPED BY THE STARS

All comedians start off as huge fans of the art form before daring to try it ourselves. As you climb the ranks, you start to rub elbows with those you admired.

It's actually surprising how accessible comedians are. Unlike a band who can practice in their garage and then reveal their new album, there's really no shortcut to practicing jokes. It simply must be done in front of small crowds before taking it to the big theaters. The audience is a major part of the process. Famous comedians don't mind popping into small local clubs that you would think they are too big for.

That's why over the years I've shared the stage with Chris Rock, Dave Chappelle, Brad Garrett, Aziz Ansari, Jay Leno, Daniel Tosh, Damon Wayans and many more. "Sharing the stage" ranges from touring several cities with a celeb to performing at 8pm while the headliner goes on at 10, unaware you were on the same show.

Sometimes you think you are about to go on stage, a big name walks through the door, and you're informed by the staff you're not going to perform after all. This is called "getting bumped" and it happens regularly. To add insult to injury, your friends and family in the crowd are more excited to see the replacement act as well!

One such night I was to perform for the owner of The Comedy Cellar. This is one of the biggest comedy venues in the world. Legends grace the stage nightly. To do well in front of the owner could change your life. Getting "passed" meant performing there regularly and could eventually lead to friendships with the best of the best, TV shows, movies, sponsorships... the sky is the limit.

My slot was right in the middle of the night. Great placement. I was to do 8 minutes of my best material while the owner watched. She came into the green room where I was waiting and said, "You may not be going on after all, but we shall see."

Just then, Ray Romano walked in the door. He had a show in a huge theater across town that same night and wanted to warmup on our stage before going off and making a few hundred thousand dollars.

The owner was happy, the other comedians were happy, everyone was happy... except me. Ray is known to be a very nice guy. He graciously said hello to all the comedians backstage and when he got to me, I joked, "*Wonderful.* Ray Romano is here on my big audition night. What could go wrong?!" He laughed, "Ahhh, gee, maybe. I can... ehh, it's gonna be tight for me to get to the next theater. Uhhh..."

I quickly jumped in, "Don't worry about it. Just giving you a hard time. Nice to meet you." At that moment he was whisked onto the stage to the surprise of the audience. He got a standing ovation for walking out. He got a standing ovation in the middle of his set. Ten minutes later he said goodnight and got yet another standing ovation. It was as if EVERYBODY *loved* Raymond.

Now, my turn. This is not ideal. Hard to stand out when a legend who's been on everyone's TV for two decades has just decimated the room.

The host jumped on stage and continued to give it up for Ray. He then quickly announced my name to a much less enthusiastic response. People were thinking, "Who?" I walked up there feeling like an empty shell of a comedian. I have no idea what I did or said. In a blur, I delivered my jokes, and said goodnight. Luckily the audience was still gracious. They gave a lot of laughs and while it was no Romano-sized response, the owner told me I was welcome to call in my avails and perform on her stage from that point forward. Little moments like this put you in the pressure cooker. It is why now after 16+ years in the business, when people ask, "So are you nervous to perform tonight for my group of insurance agents?" The answer is a resounding, "NO."

LAST COMIC STANDING

NBC offered a TV show for up-and-coming comedians that helped launch a lot of careers. Sadly, the hit show came to an end before I could make it on.

After a long hiatus, Wanda Sykes stepped in and convinced the network to do one more season of *Last Comic Standing*. With no agent or connections, I had no choice but to send an email with links to my clips through NBC's general website. What are the chances anyone even sees this?

Surprise! Two months later a response came informing me LA auditions were full, but if I wanted to fly to San Francisco on my own dime, I could get on a showcase up there. I cleared my schedule and made that happen.

The night of the showcase I was pacing backstage with other comedians who I'd met over the years. They asked which jokes I planned to do. I'm not exactly the most PC comedian on earth. After revealing my setlist they said, "Ehh, might not want to try those in *San Francisco* if I were you."

Now they had me second-guessing the tastes of a Bay Area audience. To make matters worse, I was set to go first. This always happens to me on major showcases and competitions. The sweet spots in the middle of the show always go to the ones with the best agents and representation. (They call the first spot "taking the bullet", but I've been forced to do it so often, I've learned how to thrive in that position and can usually create a big problem for the next few comedians to follow.)

Deciding to stick to my guns I did my signature jokes, demonstrating out how by turning my wrists outward I look gay, and when I bring my wrists back to a regular position it magically goes away. The crowd howled. I informed them I had 3 gay roommates and my friends were worried that I might turn gay under these conditions. I joked, "They're roommates not vampires. They don't sneak in my room like Dracula muttering, "I vantttt to suckkkk your... you-know-vhattttt."

Big laughs. I returned home to an email. I'd made it to yet *another* showcase, but in LA this time.

Then I was informed that sadly, *Last Comic Standing* had been cancelled.

Then I got a phone call that the show just might be back on but hold tight. What was going on? The Hollywood emotional roller-coaster was taking its toll.

By the time I finally went in for the next audition I was jaded. I took the stage with only 12 people in the crowd. Someone sat in a dark corner booth jotting down notes. It seemed like they may have laughed at my jokes a couple of times, but who knows. At the conclusion of my showcase, the producer asked if I would please share just how much it would mean to me to get on *Last Comic Standing*.

Instead of pander, I kind of shrugged it off, "You know, I'm like a working comedian now. You guys have passed on me for 10 years. It'd be a great experience but it's not going to ruin my life if it doesn't happen. I have a lot of other shows and events lined up. Either way, I'm fine."

With that, I walked off. Probably not the absolute best way to word that. Turns out the person in the shadows was Wanda Sykes. She's known for her brutal honesty, so perhaps this type of answer appealed to her because *I was selected for the show!*

Instead of the typical 20 episodes it was reduced to only 5. This meant after each round they'd have to cut more comedians than ever before.

ROUND 1:

100 comedians. We faced off knowing only 25 would make it out of there.

I hit them with my best jokes while celebrity judges Roseanne, Norm MacDonald, and Keenan Ivory Wayans watched. Anthony Jeselnik stepped on stage to ask them what they thought. The judges gave three thumbs up. I was going to the next round.

ROUND 2:

The remaining comedians were there to compete and only 10 would be allowed to stay. I was selected to take the stage... you guessed it – FIRST.

With years of preparation, I packed it all into a nice tight 4 minutes. Thumbs up from all three judges. The next few comedians were told to go home. The comedian after that benefited from only needing to be slightly funny as the audience was rooting for someone, *anyone* to pop at this point. She did just that with an "okay" set. The rest were hit-or-miss for the rest of the night.

When the TOP 10 finalists were announced, it looked like a perfectly cast magazine ad: 3 Blacks, 3 Whites, 2 Asians, 2 Latinos, and a Partridge in a Pear Tree. (Some standing in the winner's circle had even received criticism from the celebrity judges that they weren't quite ready and needed to work on their act.)

It appeared ½ Persian didn't register as a "minority of choice" once again. We really have to market this better.

Not to worry. Once the show aired those two performances were well received and tour dates poured in.

1/2 PERSIAN'S GOT TALENT

My next opportunity with NBC was a bit of a heartbreaker. I was able to snag an audition on *America's Got Talent*. They liked my demo clip so much they moved me straight to the taping in the Kodak Theater.

This epic 2,000+ seater is the same one they film the Academy Awards in. Backstage they have kids practicing backflips, guys preparing to spit fire, women hanging from the rafters by their hair, and singers yodeling in the hallway. *AGT* is the type of showcase where you never have any idea who might make it to the final round.

Nick Cannon grabbed me for a pre-interview. Next thing I know I'm facing Heidi Klum, Howie Mandel, Scary Spice, and Howard Stern. They ask me what I'm here to do. I joke, "I'm actually here to ask Heidi on a date." The crowd laughed. The supermodel was famously single and had just been in the tabloids for dating a 24-year-old personal trainer. Howard Stern quipped, "I think you might be too old for her!"

I said, "In that case, I'm a comedian and I'm here to make you laugh."

Heidi said, "Okay K-von, let's see what you got."

With that, I had 90 seconds to prove myself against all the ventriloquists, trampoline artists, and magicians.

I nailed the jokes, took a bow, and it went to the judges. 'Yes' from Howard Stern. 'Yes' from Scary Spice. 'Yes' from Heidi Klum. Then Howie Mandel said, "I have to be honest. I didn't like it. The crowd groaned. Then he stood up and sang, "I LOVED ITTTTTTT!"

OMG! I'd just pleased all four judges and with that, Nick Cannon rushed me backstage to ask how I felt.

"You did it. You're going to New York!"

Finally, a platform that could change everything. Cloud nine the whole way home.

Over the next week, I was informed that although it went well, they still had 4 more tapings to go and it was not guaranteed that I'd be going to New York.

"Um, there must be some mistake. I was told I'M GOING TO NEW YORK."

The producer explained that was "for the cameras," but they would make the final decision later. UGHHHHH.

Sure enough, they decided to go with a more "diverse" comedian with a hard-luck story so that America could feel bad and root for them at the same time. That's why I now call the show *America's Got Sob Stories.*

This never hit the airwaves, so there is no way to prove any of this ever happened. You just have to take my word for it, right?

Wrong! To my surprise, somebody special way in the back had broken a few rules and recorded my performance with their phone. It's easy for a comedian to lie about things, but now I had proof. I was recently able to post this lost treasure online and my fans laughed, cheered, and commiserated with me in the comments. Sure, I'm the size of an ant on the screen, and the audio has some issues, but you can clearly hear me winning over the celebrity judges and the fans that night.

Feel free to watch it online by searching: "K-von America's Got Talent." You will love it.

It just goes to show, no matter how many let downs or missed opportunities you face, keep showing up every day, do your best and great things will eventually happen. Nothing made that more obvious than the Covid-19 lockdowns.

PANPANIC

After months of hype, the newscasters came on and announced a new virus had arrived in the USA. We would all be locking down for our own safety.

I was in Hawaii, March of 2020, taking one week off before making my way across the USA to perform in dozens of Persian New Year shows. Suddenly, one by one they began canceling on me.

I've never been sad and in Hawaii at the same time. In the course of a weekend I learned that I would lose my income for the unforeseeable future.

The government labeled comedians *"Non-Essential"*. That really hurt. My brother is a doctor, so he kept his job. My mom, a nurse, so she got to keep hers. And I was forced to be this total loser. I felt like the Hunter Biden of my family.

To make matters worse, I was in the process of buying a home. This kept me from filing for those nifty government programs people were abusing. A change in income status would jeopardize the loan. I was stuck. Instead, I took odd jobs, attempted Zoom comedy shows, and sold everything I didn't need online.

What does a comedian do when there are no shows, no money coming in, and they no longer have a purpose? I never had to consider this. The first step was cut costs. I lowered my health insurance to the point that my primary physician was now listed under Veterinarians. He suggested I get neutered. One time I told him I wasn't feeling well; he put a cone on my head and told me to "Stop licking." You know what it's like to see a veterinarian for your medical advice...? ROUGH!

By the time I got a real doctor he didn't want to meet with me. He only wanted to utilize the new "Telemedicine" option and conduct our appointment over the computer. How was that going to work, this was my yearly physical exam? I was worried he would instruct me to grab my own balls and cough. (Which I do every morning but not in a clinical way.) I have no idea what I'm checking for. I also feel bad for the female patients he sees. Are they forced to place their iPad on the floor and just hover over it? Or get the ring light out? I'm guessing some women will want to add a filter so it sparkles, glitters, and glows. (Whatever it is, just don't use the one with the dog ears and the tongue that keeps popping out.)

With nothing to do, I watched the news and checked it against a wide variety of opinions online. Our leading "expert" Dr. Fauci said we do not need masks when he first spoke to the press on *60 Minutes*. His exact words, "They don't give the proper protection people think they are getting." This was probably a moment of honesty, but I'm guessing someone higher up gave him some new marching orders because 2 months later his "guidance" changed. According to Fauci, we indeed DID NEED MASKS now. The excuse we were given, "At that time there was a shortage, so we wanted to make sure only the professionals got the lifesaving masks. But now there's no shortage. You ALL NEED A MASK, or you may die." A month later Fauci was found in the baseball stands with no mask. But that's okay because he was eating a hot dog. Three months later, low and behold; Fauci recommended two to three masks would be even better, because why not, right?

People were arguing, screaming at each other, or as I call it — Mask Debating. They mask debated in public. Mask debated in private. Even mask debated at the Thanksgiving dinner table. It's no wonder the whole nation was confused. Nobody knew what was going on. We were all doing the Fauci Pokey...

> ♫ We put our masks ON
> We took our masks OFF
> We put 2 masks ON
> and we locked the country down
> We did the Fauci Pokey
> He switched his advice around
> ...Because he is a CLOWN ♫

I've already revealed that I wore masks on planes long before it was cool, so I'm no "anti-masker". However, I would wear one mask for the duration of a flight then toss it away and move on. Like a surgeon.

I would NOT demand everyone around me wear one or lose their job. I wouldn't scream at people strolling by on the beach. And I certainly wouldn't wear a mask to the gym, throw it on the floor of my car, and then wear it again the next day. Your doctor doesn't run errands in his mask, use the bathroom, do a CrossFit exercise, then come back with that same mask to finish your heart transplant.

The reality is, it says right on the box that the mask doesn't prevent viruses. Not to mention the mass population does not have a never-ending supply of fresh masks. I had the same disposable mask for ten months. By the time I finally replaced it, it was by far the dirtiest thing I owned. It wasn't stopping anything and was probably the cause of illnesses. It would have been cleaner to take off my underwear and wear that on my face.

Not to mention the tension on the ears. An orthodontist puts a small amount of pressure on your teeth for a year and it completely changes your anatomy. I want someone to measure our ears and see what long term damage was done.

The only people who liked the mask were peaceful rioters, people cheating on their spouses, and people with really ugly chins. Watch out for THOSE PEOPLE... They will lobby for mask wearing in perpetuity.

With the world in turmoil, comedy on Zoom became the thing to try. People were locked down and conducting meetings from home. Companies had a budget for Happy Hour so they would reach out and inquire about a show. This was the Wild West since nobody knew how to do a comedy show from home and now it was the only option.

These would range from great to the worst event ever. It all depended on if the people had a good sense of humor, if the company provided some good ammo on the staff, and if HR was not in on the call.

Since shows were now held over the internet, comedians were trying all kinds of things: putting an image of a brick wall behind them, talking into a wooden spoon, trying to make fun of the crowd. These things weren't working too well. It became obvious that when engaging an audience online you are no longer a stand-up, you are now hosting a show. I upgraded my camera, mic, lined up sound effects, and even offered a slide show. Might as well use all the tools of a broadcast and put on a production instead of stick to traditional comedy.

The Late-Night hosts lost their live tapings as well and found themselves in a similar position. The DIY shows were as good if not better than the network so-called superstars. It definitely balanced out the power. The pandemic became the great EQUALIZER.

This explains why my online subscribers grew 10x in such a short period. Comedy clubs were completely shut down, so I focused on my YouTube channel. With nothing else to do, I ramped up production and went from creating one video a week to five. This uncovered a whole new fan base and became one of the few positive results of the pandemic.

BACK ON TOUR

During this time, I paired up with a company called Dry Bar and we released a comedy special. They had very specific rules for the taping. We were told to refrain from bad language as well as making jokes about race, religion, politics, or sexuality. We were told not to glorify drinking or drugs. Finally, criticizing the venue was not allowed and they encouraged us to be extra cautious when talking to the crowd, but other than that, we were free to say whatever we wanted. *It's like I'd trained for this my entire life!*

Two worlds collided. The lockdown forced people indoors and this special came out at the same time. The special went viral. Fans made TikTok challenges recreating the jokes with their loved ones as they lip synced to my words. To date, the clips have gained 400+ million views and counting.

*For a big laugh be sure to search this one online: "K-von Women's Skills"

Of course, nothing beats a LIVE comedy show. After months of lockdowns, people couldn't take it anymore. The offers started coming in to perform at non-traditional venues. Comedy clubs and theaters were out, it was backyard barbecues, outdoor alleys, and basements.

Surprisingly, people had invested so much into their homes that the barns, garages, and living rooms rivaled some of the best comedy clubs in the nation.

Forget Hollywood. I realized that if I kept making meaningful videos and brought joy to people's lives, they would keep me working and make me feel essential in return.

CONCLUSION

Tanx for reading all the way to the end. Most people don't get this far! I hope you gathered some great tips and had a lot of laughs along the way.

Be sure to subscribe to my YouTube channel, tune in to the weekly podcast, and book me for your next private event.

Now if you'll excuse me, I need to go on more trips and get into more trouble so I can have more stories for the next book.

But first I'm going to ice my back, then make my way to the lobby just before the hotel ends their free breakfast, like a pro!

**K-von is the most famous Half-Persian comedian
(and now *writer)* in the world!**

He's appeared on NBC's Last Comic Standing, MTV,
and in a hilarious movie with Jon Heder (aka Napoleon
Dynamite) called *Funny Thing About Love.*

Dedicated to making people laugh, his
standup comedy clips are posted weekly & seen by
millions of people around the globe.

**Check him out on K-VONCOMEDY.COM
or his popular Youtube.com/KVONCOMEDY**

@KvonComedy on all social media

We hope you enjoyed this book.
Be sure to check out K-von's other work:

"Once You Go Persian..." (Book)
"Tanx God!" (1hr Comedy Special)
Nowruz: Lost & Found (Documentary)
"Wrists Out" (1hr Comedy Special)
"Essential" (1hr Comedy Special)